BEAUTIFUL SHRUBS

BY

ROSEMARY SHIELDS, F.R.H.S.

JOHN GIFFORD LIMITED
125, Charing Cross Road, London, W.C.2.

FIRST PUBLISHED 1946.

BOOK
PRODUCTION
WAR ECONOMY
STANDARD

Dedication

TO MY DEAR HUSBAND
WHO HAS HELPED SO MUCH

PRINTED IN GREAT BRITAIN BY
ALABASTER, PASSMORE & SONS, LTD., LONDON AND MAIDSTONE

ONLY SEEN IN COTTAGE GARDENS

. . . *"Indeed, it is impossible for any man to have any considerable Collection of noble Plants to prosper, unless he love them; for neither the goodness of the Soil, nor the advantage of the Situation, will do it, without the Master's affection . . . "*

JOHN REA, 1665.

Flora : seu de Florum Cultura.

INTRODUCTION

IN the following pages, I wish to introduce some "not so well known" beauties, which are too often strangers in the average garden. Strangers, because like lovely women, we are a little frightened of their beauty, wondering what expensive treatment, what care and cosseting they will demand ; and what tempers and peculiar characters may hide behind the beautiful faces.

I also want to re-introduce some old and well-tried friends. The old-fashioned creatures, which have been forgotten, or scorned for newer discoveries, and which, alas, are now more often than not, only seen in cottage gardens.

In offering this little book to garden lovers, it is with the hope that you may be coaxed to forget privet, laurel and ivy, and throwing caution to the winds, try something else for a hedge or wall-covering.

Oh! Privet, laurel and ivy, . . . What mournful pictures they conjure up in the mind. Pictures of leaden coloured cities on a winter's day, with dark evergreens depressingly dripping rain and grime. Of dusty cities on a summer's day, with privet coated with dust, rising from sooty-smelling earth.

Oh! The unimaginative dullness of them.

I think one of the reasons for so much unimaginative planting is that nurserymen always offer one the obvious. Whether they think one should not be trusted with the rarer beauties, or whether they cannot bear to part with them, I have never yet discovered.

Another reason is the advice given by one's neighbours. While I have many a countryman to thank for useful tips and advice, and have found most people helpful, at the same time, there are a great number of people who insist that anything unusual "won't do."

Shaking their heads, they firmly assert : "No, won't do on this soil."

By now, I have learnt to thank them politely for their advice—and as one does in matters other than gardening—promptly forget it.

I think if a plant has a reasonable chance, and that it will not definitely dislike the soil, I give it a "chance", and nine times out of ten, it "does."

This is no book for the "won't do-ers". It is for those who want to make new friends in the shrub world ; for those who wish to give their gardens, no matter how small, more character, more beauty.

One last word, to the many who have no gardens at the present time, or who have only a tiny patch.

I hope that they may find pleasure and information in these pages ; that they will find help for their plans and dreams for better and lovelier gardens in the future.

ROSEMARY SHIELDS.

Summer, 1945.

NOTE

This collection of shrubs ranges from baby creepers, twiners, climbers, and real "shrubby" shrubs, up to small trees.

After each name, I have marked D. or E. to show whether deciduous or evergreen.

In giving height, I have put that which they may be expected to reach eventually. But it must be remembered that many of them are very slow growing, and the gardener should bear in mind when ordering from a nursery, that a plant listed as ten feet, may not reach that stage for many years, and may come to him as a tiny thing of six inches or so.

The tree-heaths, for instance, are extremely slow-growing, as are the maples, and many others.

Lastly, a plant listed as "tender" or "half-hardy", is not always the delicate creature it appears. Given reasonable conditions and care, it is always worth trying.

CONTENTS

PLANNING AND ARRANGEMENT

ROSEMARY SHIELDS.

CHAPTER ONE

PLANNING AND ARRANGEMENT

THE first thing, before buying any shrubs, is to plan the garden, decide where to put them, and try to visualise how they will look.

The owner of a small garden which is overlooked by other houses, and enclosed in a fence of wire or wood, is naturally more at a disadvantage then the man with a secluded place.

But there is no possible question of doubt that it is in such a garden that shrubs play a very important part, not only in giving it character, but in giving seclusion. For no matter how much we may enjoy a chat over the fence with our neighbours, we do want part of the garden, at least, for ourselves alone.

Having decided where shrubs are to be, forget that such things as laurel, and shocking-pink papery rambler roses exist, and choose from the many beauties which abound. Indeed, it is difficult to make a choice, for each seems to have some desirable, wholly desirable attribute, and we long to have room for them all. That being impossible, we can at least fill the garden with many characters.

Instead of the old ramblers, why not *Aristolochia* (The Dutchman's Pipe)? No ordinary beauty this, but rather a quaint and amusing character, which will climb just as rapidly as a rambler, require less attention, and will decorate the walls with its queer chocolate and yellow blooms.

When planning, there are several things to be taken into consideration. Ugly walls or fences to be covered ; specimen bushes to give the garden depth and character, which one that has only flowers must necessarily lack ; taller ones for seclusion and shade ; divisions to be made between different parts of the garden, and perhaps arches and pergolas. These should always be made of wood, rough and unbarked if possible. In no circumstances should they be of metal, which is not only unsightly, but is disliked by plants.

Pillars, also made of wood, from six to ten feet high, are useful where space is restricted. They look particularly attractive along the back of wide borders, supporting roses or clematis. Or they can be used to divide off a kitchen plot.

Pergolas and arches need to be used with restraint in a small garden, but if carefully placed, they can be a great asset.

Incidentally, when possible, shrubs are better planted in groups of three or four together, especially in the case of the berried ones, which must have a male plant to fertilise the female.

When first planting, shrubs may be put fairly close together, and some removed when they become overcrowded ; or they may be spaced out, the vacant spaces filled with herbaceous plants for the first year or so.

One common fault is that too often a garden is planned with no thought for the house in its midst. Linked together by shrubs, plants and trees, there should be a happy marriage between house and garden.

PLANTING

We all know of the ''green-fingered'' people who have only to poke a plant into the earth for it to flourish like the green bay tree. But, for the ordinary mortal, it is as well to do the job properly, and to give the plant a sporting chance.

The first thing to bear in mind is that it is better to plant a small shrub than a large one. The bigger and older they are, so like old people, they seem to become attached to their surroundings, and bitterly resent any change. This applies particularly to evergreens. So don't be greedy ; go for the small chaps. The worst losses I have had with shrubs have been through greedily trying to remove very large ones.

The best time for planting deciduous shrubs is from February to March, or from October to November.

Evergreens are better moved from March to April, or from September to October. In every case, it is better when the ground is moist, but not sodden, and not, of course, frosty.

Unless the soil is very heavy, I always prefer to plant the deciduous in autumn, for then they get a good chance to establish themselves well before spring. On the other hand, evergreens seem to do better if moved in spring, just before growth has started, and in spring-planting, a mulch of light manure or straw is very helpful in protecting the roots from possible frosts, or too-drying sun and wind.

When planting a hedge, make a trench for it, and if it is against a fence or wall, keep it about eighteen inches away, to allow room for the roots. Climbers should be treated the same, as it is essential, if they are to do well, that the roots get air and moisture.

When planting, do allow space for the roots to spread out naturally. If they are cramped and squeezed into a hole, how can they be comfortable ? Like a person with too tight shoes, their life is miserable. Never use a dibber for the tiny ones, always a trowel.

Allowing space, on the other hand, does not mean a great depth. Many people make the mistake of planting shrubs too deeply. They half bury the poor things so that they can hardly breathe.

A very large shrub, such as a buddleia or rhododendron, needs about six inches of soil covering its top roots. Small ones such as heaths, etc., need about three inches. The soil mark on the stem will show to what depth the shrub was planted in the nursery garden. That mark should come just below the soil surface.

Never dig the hole until you are ready for it, for the obvious reason that in dry weather it will become parched, and in wet weather will fill with water.

If the plant has any damaged roots, cut them off with a sharp knife, cutting upward and outward.

Having dug the hole, loosen the subsoil to allow good drainage, place in the shrub, and fill in with fine soil. The roots must lie horizontally, and on no account should they hang down all in a muddle. After a layer of soil two or three inches deep has been put in, it should be trodden down, and the process continued until the hole is filled in. Prick over the top soil lightly with a fork, so that it does not cake and harden.

It is important that the shrub should be very firm, and if a stake is necessary, this should be put in before the roots are covered.

Unless the weather is very wet, always water after planting.

If plants arrive after a long journey with dried-up roots, do not, as sometimes recommended, plunge into water. This washes away the soil adhering to the roots, and it is important that they should retain as much soil as possible. Rather, put them in a "puddle" of soil and water, a fairly firm muddy mixture, and when they are removed it will stick to the roots.

As regards spacing. It depends on the size of the plants, but, approximately, dwarfs should be two to three feet apart, those of medium size three to four feet, the large ones five to six feet, and climbers should have a distance of five feet.

RESENT BEING TIGHT-LACED

14

CHAPTER TWO

TRAINING AND PRUNING

TRAINING is a simple business, but even so there is the right and wrong way to go about it. The thing to remember is that the plant should look as natural as possible. Climbers particularly, seem to suffer from too much tying up, or the other extreme of being allowed to ramble into a tangled mass.

Jasmine particularly resents "tight-lacing", and will give far better bloom if tied only just enough to support it. Clematis is often allowed to have too much freedom, and one sees it sometimes clambering over a cottage roof in an unmanageable muddle, its flowers deteriorating year by year.

The best things for tying back shrubs are soft tarred twine or strips of cloth.

I sometimes wonder if more harm is done by too much pruning than by too little. I have seen so many shrubs spoilt by harsh pruning that when I see someone looming over a plant with secateurs rampant, I am tempted to say, "Oh, woodman, spare that tree! . . ."

But, you know, it's not such a difficult job as is sometimes supposed.

In the particulars of each shrub, I have given details of pruning, but I should like here to explain the matter a little more fully.

First of all, the reason for pruning. The main reason is to encourage good blooms. It is also to allow light and air to reach the wood, and to keep the plant a neat shape.

The important thing in pruning is to know why you are doing it ; to know how and when the shrubs flower. For instance, it's no use pruning a shrub into a nice compact shape only to find that you have cut off the shoots on which the flowers were about to bloom.

There are different ways of pruning :

(*A*) Cutting back the shoots.

(*B*) Side shoots are ''spurred''. That is, cut back to leave three or four buds.

(*C*) Main shoots ''topped''. Cut back by about one-third.

(*D*) Main shoots ''tipped''. Just a little taken off to keep the plant neat.

(*E*) Disbudding, and the removal of seed heads.

The time to prune depends upon the time when the shrub is in flower.

The way to prune depends upon whether the flowers are on new or old wood.

Deciduous shrubs which bloom in early spring must not be touched until the flowers are over. Then it should be done quickly, to give the plant plenty of time to make new growth for the following year. Unless the plant is too big, or not doing well, these should only be pruned very lightly, just ''tipping'' (trimming) the ends of weak branches.

Evergreens which flower early (Garrya, etc.) should not be pruned until June. Here again, they need only very light treatment, unless you wish to make them smaller for some particular reason, as with the deciduous.

Conifers are not usually pruned, except as hedges, and they are best done in autumn.

Tender ones should never be pruned in autumn, because of the danger of frost. The work should be done in late April or May.

When flowers are borne on the *new shoots* (those of the current year), any old or weak wood should be removed, preferably in autumn.

When flowers are borne on the *old wood* (last year's

16

growth), the shrub should be pruned as soon as the flowers fade. Remove old wood, dead flowers, and trim to keep a nice shape (*i.e.* Philadelphus, ribes, the evergreen ceanothuses, etc.).

Those which flower in *late summer* on wood formed *earlier in the season* should be pruned in winter or February. They can be pruned hard back if wished, but if there is no particular reason for doing so, the shoots which have borne flowers can just be shortened (*i.e.* the deciduous ceanothuses, etc.).

Climbers

Many climbers do not require pruning and, in any case, very few of them require hard pruning. None of them should be clipped with shears except ivy. When dealing with clematis, it should be remembered that there are four groups, each needing different treatment.

(1) Montana, alpina, flammula, Armandi, paniculata, and tangutica should only have the old wood removed after flowering. If you wish them to grow big, there is no necessity to prune at all.

(2) Members of the azurae, floridæ and langinosæ groups should be pruned very lightly in February.

(3) Viticellæ and Jackmani groups need pruning hard back in winter. The whole plant may be cut back to within a foot or two of the base.

(4) Davidiana, integrifolia, necta, Pitcheri, Viorna and crispa only need the tips attending to if they have been damaged by frost. This can be done in early spring.

It will easily be understood that no hard and fast rules can be laid down for pruning shrubs. It must depend on each individual plant. In the descriptive list of shrubs I have given the requirements of each.

Staking

It should not be necessary to mention the importance of staking. Surely it is easy enough to see when a plant needs a stake ? Better still, never to allow that need to arise. I therefore mention this, because I have seen many a shrub swaying about in the wind, loosening its roots for want of a stake, and in gardens where people profess to call themselves gardeners.

It is just murder to allow them to remain in such a condition, and in fact, if they are so left, it is unlikely that they will remain long.

As already mentioned in ''planting'', when the shrub is large enough, the stake should be put in at planting time. Incidentally, try not to use a stake with bark on, as it harbours pests. If possible use a round stake which has been creosoted. A piece of sacking should be placed round the stem before it is tied up, to prevent it rubbing against the stake. Tarred cord should then be tied firmly round it, then looped round the stem to hold it in position, but not too tightly or it will cut.

OH! WOODMAN, SPARE THAT TREE!

PROPAGATION

THERE are several methods of propagation. It is an interesting part of the work, and one which should be understood, for it is essential to keep raising young plants to replace old ones, or to increase some particular favourite. It is also necessary from an economy point of view.

Of the various ways, *Grafting* and *Budding* are by far the most difficult for the amateur. Both need care and practice. It is really hardly necessary to use either method when a very satisfactory stock of shrubs may be raised by the simple ways of *Cuttings* and *Layering*.

I think too, that the easiest way to teach a person grafting and budding is by showing them. If possible, get someone to show you. Half an hour with an expert is worth a dozen volumes on the subject.

If this all sounds rather difficult, I would point out that, like many other things, it's "easy when you know how".

I have endeavoured to make the following a concise and simple explanation of the procedure.

Grafting

There are several ways of grafting, but the two which are least complicated are *Crown* (or rind), and *Whip* (or tongue) grafting.

The reason for grafting is to raise a shrub quickly, or for changing its habits (*i.e.* to graft a dwarf weeping variety on to a tall one). To add strength to those of weak habit.

The branch to be grafted is called the "scion", and the tree on which it is grafted is called the "stock".

Eventually, the stock will be the roots, and the scion will have the stem, flowers and fruits.

Grafting can only be done with plants of an allied species (*i.e.* you cannot graft a plum on to an oak).

It should be done when the sap is flowing in spring and summer. April is about the best month. The shoots which are to be grafted must be well-ripened wood, removed before growth begins in spring, and planted out in a shady border to stop them starting into growth beforehand. At the same time, the stocks should have the branches sawn off to within a few inches of where the graft is to be. The stock should be grafted as near the ground as possible. Stocks which are going to be standards must, of course, be allowed to grow to the appropriate height.

Crown (or rind) grafting is done when there is a discrepancy in size between the scion and the stock. The boughs must be sawn off where it is intended to graft, to leave a flat, smooth stump. Several vertical incisions about three inches long are made in the bark, which is loosened to open it out. The scion, which has been cut obliquely (in a wedge-like manner), is slipped inside the separated bark and bound in position. By the way, if you are putting several scions in, they must all be in position before binding.

The important layer to cause the union is the cambium layer. (Green tissues on the inside of the bark.) When the scions are bound, the whole of the cut part must be covered with grafting wax.

Tongue (or whip) grafting is used when the scion and stock are almost the same size. The stock is cut back at the place where it is to have the graft.

The scion is cut the same as for crown grafting, then it is turned round and cut again (about half-way through only) in the opposite direction. A thin piece of wood is cut from the stock, so that there is a flat surface to fit the scion. A downward cut is made to form a tongue, and the two are fitted well together. Bind carefully, and cover with grafting wax.

Budding

I think this is rather easier than grafting, although this, too, needs care and practice. It is really a form of grafting,

20

the difference being that only a bud, and not a whole shoot, is taken, and it should be done in summer when the sap is flowing fully.

Choose a shoot when the wood is firm and half ripened. The best wood is the growth of the current year.

The leaves of the shoot should be removed, but the leaf-stalk left. It is where this joins the stem that a growth bud lies dormant.

A sharp knife is then inserted about half an inch below a leaf stalk, and sliced upward to come out about half an inch above it. This portion should now be shield-shaped, somewhat resembling the base of a large rose thorn.

Now hold it by the leaf stalk, turn it over, and it will be seen to contain a piece of wood. This is lifted with the knife, then pulled away from the bark with the fingers, so that the cambium layer is shown.

Make a T-shaped incision in the bark of the stock, and lever up the bark on either side of the vertical arm of the T. The upper part of the bud must be cut across to conform with the top of the T, then it can be slipped into the separated area, and the bark replaced as far as possible over the bud. This is now bound gently but firmly into position above and below the eye, being sure to cover all the cut part.

The top of the stock is not removed as in grafting, nor is it necessary to cover it with wax.

The best time to bud is when the weather is wet. If it is dry, water the stock well two or three days beforehand.

After budding the stock must not be touched until late autumn, when the binding can be cut to allow it to grow, and the top of the stem which bears the bud can be cut back to about three inches from it. In spring it can be cut again to within about one inch of the bud, and in summer all shoots springing from the stock must be cut away.

Division

There are a certain number of shrubs which lend themselves to the easy method of propagating by division. This is carried out from November to March for the deciduous, and in October or April to May for the evergreens.

Shrubs which are suitable for this method are those which make new growth from below ground level (*i.e.* lilac, rosemary, lavender, cydonia japonica, etc.).

Those which have suckers (*i.e.* lilac) are easily divided. The suckers are just cut off with a spade, making sure they have some good roots attached.

The others are divided in the same manner as herbaceous plants. They are carefully separated with the hands, or if they prove stubborn, with two small hand forks which are dug in back to back in the middle of the root, and levered gently apart.

This is a very easy way of propagation, and of course, produces new plants quickly.

Seeds

The worst part of raising shrubs from seed is that it is such a lengthy business ; there is also the risk that a great number of inferior seedlings will turn up.

The seeds of most shrubs will germinate in a couple of months, although some take a year.

The hardy ones can be sown outside, but those of a more tender nature must go into boxes in the greenhouse.

You should gather the fruits of berried shrubs in autumn, and store them in sand in boxes. In spring, separate the seed from the enfolding covering, and plant (if hardy) outside in drills in the seed bed.

It is as well to have the seed bed raised slightly above the level of the ordinary soil, and the two most important things to do are to keep it moist in dry weather, and always free from weeds.

The seed bed should be in a sheltered, not too sunny spot,

THEY HALF BURY THE POOR THINGS

The soil, very firm, should contain a little sand. It should be pressed down firmly, well watered, and left at least a week before sowing.

The depth to sow depends, of course, on the size of the seed. Tiny ones should only just have soil lightly raked over them. The usual way is to cover them with twice their own thickness of soil. Water lightly after sowing.

When they are large enough to handle, transplant to six or eight inches apart in rows about two and a half feet apart.

The more tender ones which have to go under glass should be sown very thinly in a compost of two-thirds loam, one-third leaf mould and a little silver sand, the bottom of the box being covered well with broken crocks to ensure good drainage.

An earthenware pot is better than a box, as it keeps the soil more evenly moist than wood. After sowing, water the seeds by immersing the pot or box in water up to the rim, so that the water can soak up from the base.

Cover the boxes with glass, and then with brown paper,

which can be removed as soon as the seeds have germinated, and the glass raised a little, to allow air to enter. A few days later, when all the little plants are up, the glass may be removed.

By the way, the glass must be wiped each day, so that it does not become wet with condensation. Gradually, the boxes can be lifted nearer the glass. If this is not done, the seedlings become very straggly.

When they are about three inches high, they can be pricked off and planted about three inches apart in boxes, which are replaced about six inches from the glass, until they are ready for hardening off.

Layering

This is perhaps the easiest way of all of propagating. It can be done at any time of the year, although the best time is in spring. A very great number can be propagated this way—daphnes, rhododendrons, veronicas, etc., and of course honeysuckle, and all those with branches which can be easily bent to the soil.

Having chosen a suitable branch, you make an incision (in an upward direction), just below a joint. Press this cut part down into the soil, and peg it there with wire or wood. Cover well with soil, and tie the outer end of the shoot to a stake. This keeps it firm, and also turns it upwards so that the flow of sap is stopped.

After a few months you can remove some of the soil gently, to see how the roots are progressing, and as soon as they are good the shoot can be cut away from the plant.

In autumn, it can be planted in its permanent position.

Cuttings

This is an excellent way of propagating, for it is simple enough for a child to do, and it is very effective. It gives large plants quickly, and (as with layers) it is always certain that plants will come true to type.

The cuttings should be from four to twelve inches long,

cut off just below a joint. If you can take a heel (a small wedge-shaped piece of the old wood) with it, it helps, because it makes a larger surface on which roots can be formed. If the tips are unripened, and they usually are, they should be trimmed off with a sharp knife. It is best to take side shoots low down on the stem.

The only leaves which must be removed are those on the part of the stem which will be inserted in the soil.

The length of the cutting is usually reckoned by the space between the joints of the plant. For instance, if they are one inch apart, the cutting should be twelve inches. If they are less, the cutting can be shorter. The cuttings should be inserted four to six inches deep. This does not mean that you cannot take them smaller or larger; I must confess I often take much larger ones, and they usually do well.

Most shrubs, except the very tender ones, can be struck in the open ground, in sandy soil in a sheltered bed.

The less hardy can be struck in pots in a cold frame.

Cuttings can be taken in autumn when the wood is quite mature, in August when half-mature, or in early summer when the shoots are beginning to ripen. The deciduous are usually taken between October and February. They are generally very easy and undemanding, but some of the more tender evergreens are better given the protection of a frame.

Those inserted in autumn do not usually make roots until the spring, and they must not be moved until the following autumn.

If you have a number of cuttings to plant, the best way is to make a little trench, the bottom covered with silver sand. If the ends of the cuttings are stuck in this, they will root more quickly than if in the plain soil.

The most essential thing is to see that they are planted firmly.

HAPPY MARRIAGE BETWEEN HOUSE AND GARDEN

CHAPTER THREE

SOILS AND MANURES

BEFORE planting anything at all, it is essential to understand something about the soil. This is particularly important in the case of shrubs, many of which have most definite likes and dislikes as to where their feet are put.

For instance, Andromeda, Enkianthus, Fothergilla, Erica and Cassiope are some of those which positively hate lime, and it is hopeless to attempt to put them in it.

Supposing that you do not quite understand your soil, the best thing to do is to ask the advice of a neighbour, or the local nurseryman, and take note of what flourishes in the neighbourhood.

A rough guide to soil is that a heavy or clay soil clings to the shoes, and when wet can be moulded in the fingers. It has a slithery, greasy sort of feeling when damp. A light, sandy soil does not stick, but gives way under the feet, and it feels gritty when rubbed through the fingers.

You can also tell by the things which grow naturally in the neighbourhood. For instance, heather and rhododendrons grow in peaty soil, cowslips in clay, beech trees, king-cups and ferns in marshy lands.

It is a waste of time and money putting shrubs in soil which they are known to dislike, but at the same time, there is no need to go to the other extreme and refuse to grow them at all just because the soil is not perfect for them. Most shrubs love peat, leaf-mould and sandy loam.

Given an ordinary, even rather poor soil, a good bed can be made up for them of suitable material. This, plus a yearly top-dressing of leaf-mould, will deceive them sufficiently to make them flourish quite happily.

It must also be remembered that there are a very great number which are perfectly content in an ordinary soil, and there is no need to think that shrubs are difficult or fussy. Indeed, very few of them can be termed "fussy".

Incidentally, most gardeners and gardening books talk very lightly of "loam", but the beginner does not always know exactly what it is. Loam is the perfect mixture of light and heavy soil. A good example is the thick top spit of field grass that has been stacked for a considerable time until it is well rotted. If you are fortunate enough to be able to dig it from a meadow yourself, you should take it about five inches deep, and make it all into a stack, with the grass side downwards so that it will rot. It should be left like that for at least a year before being used. When the loam is "light", it contains more sand, and when "heavy", it contains more clay.

Peat is usually lacking in lime, and for that reason is beloved by Ericas, Azaleas, etc. Peat, unfortunately, usually has to be bought, unless one lives in a peaty place such as Hampshire. It is made up of decayed vegetable matter, old roots and sand.

Leaf-mould is formed of decayed leaves. These are piled in a heap and turned occasionally, until they become a dark, broken-up mould. Oak and beech leaves are the best.

Humus is the decayed vegetable and animal matter. (Lawn mowings, hay, straw, vegetable refuse, etc.) It is absolutely essential for making the soil really good, and no artificial fertiliser can take its place.

A certain amount of lime is necessary in all soils. It makes heavy soil more porous, cleans it of pests, and stops it from becoming sour. It must never be used at the same time as animal manure. Slaked lime is best for heavy soils, and carbonate of lime for light and sandy soils.

28

The best of all manures is, of course, stable or farmyard. If this is unobtainable, artificials must be used, but of course they do not affect the tilth of the soil, and they do not add humus.

Three plant foods are needed by soil :—

Nitrogen, to make good growth of leaves, shoots, etc.

Potash, to improve the colour and size of blooms.

Phosphates, to help the development of fruit, seed and root.

There are many good fertilisers on the market these days, and most are described and explained on the packages, so that it is unnecessary to go into more detail here. Some of them contain nitrogen, potash and phosphates all ready mixed in the correct proportions, which is as good a way as any to buy them.

A brief guide to soils in general is as follows :—

Calcareous soil contains about twenty per cent. or more of lime, with sand or clay loam, and a little humus.

Clay soil has about fifty per cent. stiff clay, with a little sand, and lacks lime and humus.

Loamy soil has from twenty to thirty per cent. clay, the rest being sand, lime and humus.

In sandy loam, the largest proportion is sand ; in calcareous loam, it is lime ; in gravel loam, gravel ; and in chalk loam, chalk.

Marly soils are decomposed limestone rock containing five to twenty per cent. carbonate of lime and humus. They are divided into Argillaceous, loamy and sandy marls, according to the predominance of clay, loam or sand.

Peaty soil is the richest and best of all. It contains twelve or more per cent. humus, and sand and fibrous vegetable matter.

Sandy soil contains about eighty per cent. sand, with some clay, lime and a little humus. Sandy soil is usually poorest by the seaside. Here, seaweed plays a very important part, for liberal application will greatly improve the lightness of the soil.

FRIENDS AND FOES

The most unpleasant part of gardening, without any doubt, is the "pest" part.

Fortunately, shrubs suffer less from the onslaught of pests than many other things. After constant battles in the kitchen garden with weevils and "what-nots" of every description, it is a relief to turn to the shrubs. Not that they are a race apart, bearing a charmed life, for almost any season you can come upon blobs of cuckoo spit and signs of numerous destructive little creatures here and there. But, if it be any consolation, at least they haven't such unpleasant names as the enemies of the kitchen garden. Maggots and weevils, for instance ! You could almost, almost forgive the sinners for the charming names they bear. For instance, Little Ermine Moth. I always imagine a regal

30

little chap clad in a cloak of ermine, and wearing a gold coronet, as he sets out for a tasty dinner of Euonymus.

While the Laburnum Miner, on the other hand, must be more of a working man in rough cloth, with a lamp and a pick for his work on the golden laburnums.

But to return to the nastier ones. I suppose the slugs and snails do as much damage to shrubs as almost anything. They are very fond of young juicy shoots. Slugs are particularly fond of young clematis, and they certainly do a great deal of damage.

They seem to differ in different soils. In some parts, the great black slimy-looking slug seems to reign supreme. In others, the shell-snail abouds, while in others there appears to be a flourishing community of greys, browns, mauves, mottled, dappled and striped, penny plain, twopence coloured.

They are at their worst on mild spring and early summer nights, and one of the best ways of dealing with them is to put down little heaps of bran or some other slug-bait in the morning, and in the evening about ten o'clock, take a torch and go round collecting them. Take something to lift them with, and drop them in an old box, then drown them with boiling water.

The shrubs should, of course, be protected by a barrier of soot or fresh lime four or five inches wide round them.

By the way, I would just mention, for those who are tender-hearted about killing slugs, snails, ants, caterpillars, etc., that they may be exterminated with a clear conscience, for they do not feel pain.

After dealing with slugs and snails (principally in spring and early summer), we come to the caterpillars, which will probably keep us busy from spring until autumn.

There are all sorts of caterpillars and grubs, and they are best picked off the shrub (often found in a curled-up leaf) and squashed between finger and thumb, or if this is too distasteful, squashed between two stones.

These grubs and caterpillars can do quite a lot of damage to shrubs, what with weaving cocoons and little homes for themselves out of the most tender leaves, and feeding greedily on the choicest buds and leaves.

It is quite impossible for the amateur to distinguish one caterpillar from another, except for a few of the more common, but this does not matter much, as they should all be killed. The moths which produce these creatures are more easily recognised.

The Little Ermine Moth, which is particularly fond of Euonymus and mountain ash, is very pretty, clad in white or dove grey, with little black dots like ermine tails.

THE LITTLE ERMINE MOTH

The Tortrix Moth has a very large family which includes the Red Rose Maggot, the Allied Tortrix, Tortrix podana, and many others. They are all small creatures, never more than three quarters of an inch across the wings. The Red Rose Moth is a smoky-grey brown with grey underwings. The Allied Tortrix has red-brown front wings, and grey hind wings with a tiny yellow fringe. Tortrix podana has brown front wings with a faint rosy sheen, and the hind wings are yellow. All these moths are fond of roses, lilacs, etc.

The Swallow Tail Moth is a pale yellow with darker lines. It is very fond of honeysuckle, elder and ivy.

The Winter Moth attacks roses and many other shrubs, besides being a fruit pest. The females are queer little things, pale grey, with six long legs and tiny little wings. The males are larger, yellow-brown, with paler hind wings.

The Vapourer Moth is particularly injurious to roses, and it also attacks various shrubs. The male is a lovely chestnut colour with darker markings. The female is a plump little grey thing without wings. The caterpillars are very pretty, being dark grey, spotted with red, and tufted on the back with yellow and brown hairs.

Cuckoo Spit is the frothy white stuff sometimes called Frog Hopper Insect. Before they are able to hop, they live in the frothy stuff, and suck the sap of the plant. The cuckoo spit insect is yellowish brown and very small. It is very active from July to October.

The Mottled Umber Moth attacks roses, privet, lilac, philadelphus, etc. The female is a brown wingless, beetle-like thing, but the male is a very attractive pale amber with wavy markings, and paler hind wings.

One way to deal with all these pests is to pick off any cocoons or caterpillars and burn them, or drown them in boiling water. Better still, spray with some good wash. Paraffin is often advised, but I do not like it, for it can be harmful to delicate shrubs, and I do not advise it except in rare cases.

One of the best washes for greenfly is half a pound of soap and one pound of quassia to ten gallons of water.

For cuckoo spit, leaf-hoppers and maggots, a nicotine wash is the best thing.

Of course, the moths themselves should always be destroyed. They will often be found on fences or shady walls.

B

When spraying, remember, if it is for aphis, cuckoo spit or rose maggot, the spray must be heavy, covering every part, until all the leaves drip. But if for caterpillars, the spray must be very fine, and cover all the foliage, top and underneath, so that whatever they eat is poisoned.

Never spray in the sun, or it will scorch the leaves, nor on a cold evening. Try not to spray on fully opened blooms, or it may stain them.

Lastly, be cheered by the good friends of the garden. The toads and frogs, which live on many of the enemies. The centipede, which eats soil grubs (not to be confused with the millepede or the wireworm). The centipede always scurries along as if in a hurry, and has a pair of legs to each section of its body. The bright little ladybird, which obligingly eats green-flies, black-flies, etc. The birds, which, with the exception of the house-sparrow, pigeons, and sometimes jays, do far less harm than good.

Many people have a mistaken idea that birds are enemies. Indeed they are not ; they are ardent gardeners, destroying snails, slugs, caterpillars, and numerous insects. Even the annoying little house-sparrow takes its toll of insects and grubs. Without the birds, the tits, the wrens, the thrushes, and many others, the garden would be in a bad way, from every point of view, and if they take a little payment in the way of a few peas, or juicy young shoots, or fruit, they have earned it well.

The best attitude to adopt towards pests is to take reasonable precautions against them, destroy them when you see them, and not to fuss too much, or to lose any sleep wondering what harm they are doing in your absence.

Many a season goes by with hardly the sight of a snail, or the sound of a moth wing at dusk ; all seem to have departed to other gardens, and it is for you to take your leisure, and for other gardeners to get busy with baits, and traps, and washes.

LOVELIEST OF ALL . . . THE FRAGRANT

CHAPTER FOUR

LOVELIEST OF ALL . . . THE FRAGRANT

O F all beautiful shrubs, surely there can be no question of doubt that the loveliest are the fragrant.

I would rather have some of the modest little white or yellow blossoms which yield such delectable sweetness to the air than any of the flamboyant, brilliant beauties which may delight the eye with colour, but which have no scent.

Who would change the common honeysuckle as a climber against the house for the most beautiful but scentless clematis ? Or the heavenly Mock Orange or Sweet Briar for the brightest rhododendron which lacks perfume ?

Admittedly, those which possess the loveliest scents are often insignificant and modestly arrayed, and perhaps because of that they have been especially blessed by Heaven.

THE FRAGRANT

Abelia triflora (D). A charming member of the honey-suckle family, bearing long clusters of creamy-pink flowers, and having an attractive scent. Flowering in June, it grows about 12 ft. high, is half-hardy, and needs a warm, sheltered wall. For soil, it prefers equal parts of peat, loam and sand, and good drainage. It will also do in a good ordinary soil.

Prune: lightly after flowering.

Propagate: layers in spring.

Actinidia polygama (D). This lovely climber has clusters

36

of wax-white blossoms, which are particularly fragrant at the close of day. It is hardy, and will uncomplainingly clothe a north wall, or trellis or tree stumps in exposed positions. It flowers in summer, and is happy in any ordinary soil.

Prune: not necessary.

Propagate: layers in autumn.

Akebia quinata (E). Though not suitable for outdoors in the north, it will thrive against a south wall in the southern and western counties. It is well worth a little care, for it has very fragrant dark violet, magnolia-like flowers, set off by glossy leaves. It will grow up to 30 ft. It prefers a deep moist, loamy soil.

Prune: straggly shoots after flowering.

Propagate: layers in autumn.

Amorpha fruticosa (Bastard Indigo) (D). Has spikes of lovely blue-purple, scented flowers. Very hardy ; flowers in July, and reaches 6 ft. It is happy in any ordinary soil.

Prune: after flowering.

Propagate: cuttings in autumn, or layering in summer.

Artemisia abrotanum (Southernwood, Old Man, Lad's Love) (E). The delicate spicy scent of this old-fashioned shrub is said to keep moths out of clothes. It has delightful feathery foliage, grows to about 4 ft., is hardy, and will do anywhere. A garden always seems to me incomplete without it. The little yellow flowers appear in August.

Prune: not necessary.

Propagate: cuttings in autjmn.

Azalea. *See* Rhododendron.

Azara dentata (E). This hardy climber has rather insignificant flowers, but they are extremely fragrant with a vanilla-like scent. Its little pale yellow flowers appear in June, and it grows to about 10 ft. A position against a south wall is best if possible, in any ordinary soil.

Prune: not necessary.

Propagate: cuttings in spring.

Berberis (Barberry, Jaundice Berry) (E and D). Of the many beautiful Barberries from which to chose, *B. buxifolia* must not be omitted for its delightful fragrance like hyacinths. It has yellow blossoms in March and, later, purple berries. It grows about 6 to 10 ft. *B. japonica Bealei* has yellow flowers in February, which smell of lily of the valley. This grows the same height, and both are evergreens. They are hardy and not particular about soil, sun or shade.

Prune: not necessary.

Propagate: cuttings in autumn.

Buddleia variabilis magnifica (Orange Ball Tree) (E). This is a beauty to grow against a wall, with its wealth of deep violet blooms in summer. It grows about 10 ft., and will repay by cutting back to within about ten inches of the base in March. It will grow in any ordinary soil.

Prune: as above.

Propagate: cuttings in autumn.

Calycanthus floridus (Carolina Allspice) (D). A lovely shrub with dusky purple-red flowers smelling of ripe melon. Blooms May and June, and does best against south or west walls. Grows about 5 ft., and prefers peat, leaf mould, and a moist, partly shaded position.

Prune: cut out dead wood after flowering.

Propagate: layering in August.

Carpenteria californica (Californian Mock Orange) (D). In June it bears clusters of ivory flowers with golden stamens, and is one of the most fragrant shrubs. It is hardy, grows about 4 ft., and for preference would choose a light loamy soil.

Prune: the shoots which have flowered should be pruned when the blossoms are over.

Propagate: cuttings in April of layering in autumn.

Ceanothus (Mountain Sweet, Californian Lilac) (E and D). These very beautiful relatives of the Buckthorns may perhaps be regarded as unscented, but I think they deserve a place among the "fragrant". I remember *C. thyrsiflorus*, an evergreen, covering the front of a white cottage with a mantle of blue. In summer there came from it the fragile fragrance of cowslips, and it was much loved by bees. It grew about 20 ft. It was quite hardy and happy in ordinary soil.

Prune: only weak wood need be taken out in spring.

Propagate: by cuttings in autumn.

Chimonanthus fragrans (Winter Sweet, Japanese Allspice) (D). This beautiful winter flowerer should be in every garden. The starry yellow blossoms appear before the leaves, and are lovely against the slender dark branches. It grows up to 10 ft., very hardy, but does best in a rich sandy soil. Its fragrance is unmatched.

Prune: cut away shoots which have flowered in February.

Propagation: layering in autumn.

Chionanthus retusa (Fringe Tree, Snow-flower) (D). Another hardy beauty with starry white flowers, delicately perfumed. Blooms in June, and grows 6 to 8 ft. Prefers a sandy loam, and a rather moist position.

Prune: not necessary.

Propagation: budding in July.

Choisya ternata (Mexican Orange Flower) (E). This shrub bears large clusters of pure white blossoms, scented rather like hawthorn. It flowers in summer and grows 6 ft. It does best in a peaty soil.

Prune: lightly after flowering.

Propagate: cuttings March to June.

Cistus (Rock Rose, Gum Cistus) (E). There are many beautiful species, but *C. ladaniferus* is perhaps the most attractive with its white and maroon flowers which smell of attar of roses. They are easy to grow and do well on sand and lime rubble in sun.

Prune: remove dead blooms only.

Propagate: cuttings in autumn.

Clematis (Virgin's Bower, Traveller's Joy) (D and E). Few of these beautiful hardy climbers are really fragrant, but *C. cirrhosa*, an evergreen, winter-flowering, has a sweet faint perfume in its white blossoms, and *C. flammula*, a deciduous, with white flowers in autumn has a very charming fragrance. Of the herbaceous species, *C. heracleæfolia davidiana* is a charming lavender-blue, and fragrant. They all prefer their faces in the sun and their roots shaded, and a rich, well-drained loam containing old mortar and well-decayed manure.

Prune: see chapter on pruning.

Propagate: layering in summer; division in autumn.

Clerodendron trichotomum (Glory Tree) (D). This shrub is not so well known as it might be, for it bears white scented flowers in August, and later beautiful turquoise blue berries. It is quite hardy, but a warm, sheltered spot is preferable for it. It grows about 12 ft.

Prune: shoots after flowering.

Propagate: cuttings in early spring.

Clethra alnifolia (Sweet Pepper Bush) (E). The white flowers in August are very fragrant, and well set off by dark green leaves. It is hardy, reaches 8 ft., and will do in any ordinary soil. It makes a picture of bloom in late summer, and can be grown against a wall or in the open.

Prune: not necessary.

Propagate: layering in autumn.

Comptonia asplenifolia (Sweet Fern) (D). A hardy little shrub, useful for shady places. (Syn. *Myrica asplenifolia*.) Its fragile ferny foliage has a rich spicy odour when touched. It grows 2 to 4 ft. and prefers a peaty loam.

Prune: not necessary.

Propagate: layering early spring.

Corylopsis (D). Of these very hardy useful shrubs, *C. pauciflora*, slender-shaped, has scented pale yellow flowers

40

in April. Grows 8 to 10 ft., prefers open position in sandy loam, and moisture. *C. spicata* and *C. veitchiana*, also yellow and fragrant, are well worth having. They grow 3 to 4 ft.

Prune: not necessary.

Propagation: layering in autumn.

Cratægus (May, Hawthorn, Quick, etc.) (D and E). All these are fragrant, and with a particular character of their own. They are so much part of the English countryside, so typical of England in her summer gown, all fresh and fragrant.

They are very useful for any position, any soil, and any place where other shrubs are too fussy to grow. The evergreens seem to do best against walls.

C. Azarolus gives forth its white flowery fragrance in May, as does *C. monogyna* (Hawthorn), and *C. oxyacantha* (Common Hawthorn) and *C. coccinea* (Scarlet Thorn). They all grow from 15 to 25 ft.

Prune: in November merely to keep good shape.

Propagate: budding in July, grafting in March.

Cytisus (Broom) (D and E). Of the infinite variety of the delightful brooms, there is none with a more potent honey-scent than *C. scoparius*, the Common Broom. While *C. albus*, the Spanish Broom, with its cloud of moon-white bloom, ladens the air with the sweet rich smell of coconut. There are so many beautiful brooms, so many lovely hybrids, each with its own individual scent, that it is difficult to choose. The best way, if possible, is to visit a nursery garden and make a choice when they are in flower. They are all perfectly easy to grow, and will do in shrubberies, on banks, woodlands, etc.

Prune: directly after flowering, shortening old shoots.

Propagate: cuttings in August, or seeds in spring.

Daphne (Garland Flower, Spurge Laurel) (D and E). All the daphnes are charming and deliciously scented. Although

41

they are modestly gowned, they are a delight in the young year when colours and scents are scarce. Of all shrubs, both small and large, surely the daphne is one of the most beautiful ? Its profusion of perfect little blossoms covering the slender stems makes a perfect picture. The well-known *D. mezereum*, one of the best of the deciduous, has its branches laden with purplish-red blooms in February, and grows 3 to 6 ft. Of the evergreens, *D. pontica*, with its greeny-yellow flowers in April, is charming. It grows 2 to 4 ft., and is good for planting in a shrubbery, or under trees, for it does not mind drips. It is impossible to choose the nicest of the daphnes, for they are all exquisite.

Prune: not necessary.

Propagate: layering in autumn.

Datura (Thorn Apple, Trumpet Flower) (D). *D. suaveolens* has white fragrant flowers in August, and grows 8 to 10 ft. It is an attractive shrub, and will do well in any good ordinary soil, preferably in a fairly sunny position. They are only half-hardy, Some people remove the plants to the safety of the greenhouse in autumn, but I have not found this necessary in a sheltered spot, especially if they are protected in winter with matting.

Prune: freely in autumn.

Propagate: cuttings spring or autumn.

Decumaria barbara (D). This hardy climber is not a common sight in the average garden, but it is well worth growing against a house wall, for its bunches of white blooms in June are strongly scented like hawthorn. It is a twiner, and needs trellis to support its shoots. It will grow up to 20 ft. and likes a light rich soil.

Prune: weak shoots in February.

Propagate: cuttings in summer.

Drimis Winterii (D). This is a very beautiful relation of the Magnolias, and should indeed have a place in the garden if space will permit. It has flowers of an ivory-white pallor in April, and will grow from about 12 ft. to as much as 30 ft. It likes a good loamy soil, in a warm, sheltered border.

Prune: not necessary.

Propagate: cuttings in autumn.

Elæagnus (Wild Olive, Oleaster) (E and D). These are useful shrubs, for they are easy to grow and hardy. They produce their little yellow flowers in great abundance from spring to summer. Of the evergreens, *E. pungens aureomaculata* is rather attractive, for it has leaves variegated with gold. Of the deciduous, *E. augustifolius* grows about 15 ft. and has yellow flowers, and the pale green leaves are silvered underneath, and *E. argentea*, also with clusters of yellow flowers and leaves powdered with silver. They thrive in ordinary soil in open borders or against a south wall.

Prune: not necessary.

Propagate: cuttings in autumn.

Erica (Heather) (E). Of the large and fascinating family of heaths, *E. arborea* is worth noting for the lovely hawthornlike scent of its white flowers. This is a tree heath, and if happy in a sunny, sheltered place, will grow up to 6 ft. in about three years. It prefers sandy peat.

Prune: tidy straggly shoots in April.

Propagate: division in autumn, layering in spring.

Escallonia (Chilian Gum Box) (E and D). These do particularly well at the seaside, and there are several charming species well worth planting as hedges. *E. macrantha* has crimson flowers in June, and a rich green foliage which is scented when pressed. They like a well-drained ordinary soil.

Prune: tidy straggly shoots only, in spring.

Propagate: cuttings in early autumn.

Eucalyptus (Australian Gum, Blue Gum) (E). Although half-hardy, they will do well in any warm, sheltered position in the south of England. They make a very attractive picture with their bluish foliage, which is very fragrant. *E. globulus* and *E. Gunni* are both suitable for outdoor culture, and will reach about 15 ft. It is as well to give them some sort of protection in a hard winter. Any ordinary good soil suits them.

Prune: not necessary.

Propagate: seeds in spring in greenhouse.

Forsythia (Japanese Golden Bell Tree) (D). It always looks at its best if planted on a height, to show off its graceful drooping sprays. *F. suspensa* and *F. viridissima* are both a clear yellow with a very delicate scent. They both bloom in March. The former reaches 8 ft. or so, and is better grown as a climber ; the latter is more bushy, and both are hardy. They will thrive in ordinary soil and do not mind shade.

Prune: lightly after flowering.

Propagate: cuttings July and August.

Fothergilla (American Witch Hazel) (D). *F. Gardeni* (syn. *F. alnifolia*) is white and very fragrant. It flowers in May, grows about 4 to 6 ft. and absolutely hates lime. It does best in a well-drained sandy peat.

Prune: lightly after flowering.

Propagate: layering in autumn.

Gelsemium (Carolina Yellow Jessamine) (E). This half-hardy climber bears wreaths of bright yellow flowers all the summer. *G. sempervirens* (syn. *G. nitidum*). It likes a well-drained sandy loam.

Prune: not necessary.

Propagate: cuttings July and August.

Genista (Needle Furze, Petty Whin) (D). These shrubs are most useful, easy to grow, and hardy. Cousins of the brooms, they revel in sun, dry banks and light soil. *G. hispanica* (The Spanish Gorse) makes a nice little compact bush of rich yellow flowers, which appear in May. It grows 1½ ft. high.

Prune: after flowering, trim.

Propagate: layering in autumn.

Gordonia pubescens (D). This beauty is not often seen in the ordinary garden. Certainly it is half-hardy, but] if planted in a sheltered position, or against a south wall, it should give no trouble, and it can be protected in a very severe winter. Its beautiful white flowers, like camellias, appear in summer, and fill the air with their fragrance. Grows 5 or 6 ft., and prefers peat and leaf mould.

Prune: not necessary.

Propagate: layering in spring.

Hakea suaveolens (E). This will only "do" in a sheltered part of the south of England, being rather tender, and needing protection in winter. In spring it bears very fragrant white flowers, and grows up to 10 ft. Fibrous loam and leaf mould are best for it.

Prune: not necessary.

Propagate: cuttings in July.

Hamamelis mollis (Witch Hazel) (D). With its lovely scent of primroses, and its bare branches covered with little golden flowers, it is a beauty in January and February, when there is little colour in the garden. It is hardy, but likes a deep rich soil, and preferably a damp place.

Prune: lightly into shape in February.

Propagate: layering in autumn.

Heteromelles Arbutifolia (Tollon) (E). (Syn. *Photinia Arbutifolia*.) It has white scented flowers in August, and will grow up to 15 ft. It is half-hardy, and may need protection in severe weather. A well-drained loam suits it.

Propagate: cuttings July.

Hydrangea (D). Of the many beautiful hydrangeas, the only one that is really fragrant is *H. arborescens*, which is white, and grows 4 to 6 ft. Blooms in summer, thrives in any ordinary well-drained soil.

Prune: previous year's shoots to within one inch of base in February.

Propagate: cuttings in August.

Idesia polycarpa (D). A very beautiful little tree growing about 15 ft. There are male and female. The former have deep yellow flowers, and the latter pale yellow-green blossoms which are very fragrant. The leaves are bright and heart-shaped. They are hardy, and will do in any ordinary soil.

Prune: lightly after flowering.

Propagate: cuttings in March or autumn.

Itea virginica (Virginian Willow) (D). A graceful shrub with white, well-scented flowers in July, growing about 4 to 6 ft. A good position for it is a moist, sheltered shrubbery with peaty soil. In autumn the stems and foliage turn a beautiful red.

Prune: lightly after flowering.

Propagate: layering in August.

Jasminum officinale (Jasmine, Jessamine) (D). An old favourite, and well worth a place in every garden for its delicate deliciously scented white flowers. Incidentally, a common fault is to tie Jasmines back too tightly. They will bloom far better if they are only tied just enough to support them and keep them in position. *J. nudiflorum* is a bright starry yellow from October to February, and grows 10 to 14 ft. They are happy in any ordinary soil.

Prune: very moderately after flowering.

Propagate: cuttings in autumn.

Laburnum vulgare (Golden Chain) (D). Another well-known and hardy beauty, which can be shown to great advantage if trained over arches or pergolas. Its cascades of bright gold in spring have a very delicate honey scent, and it reaches 20 to 30 ft. Thrives in any soil.

Prune: lightly after flowering.

Propagate: layering autumn.

Lavandula vera (Lavender) (E). No garden should be without this old-fashioned friend, and the older the plant the richer its scent. It is invaluable for pot-pourri, or for placing in sachets and among linen. There are many charming species, but I would choose *L. vera*, for its beautiful colour. It flowers July to August in any ordinary soil, and prefers sunshine. Grows 3 ft.

Prune: shape in March.

Propagate: cuttings in September.

Ledum (Labrador Tree, Marsh Rosemary) (E). *L. palustre* has white flowers in May, and when bruised the leaves are very fragrant. It grows in ordinary soil.

Prune: not necessary.

Propagate: layering or division in September.

Leptospermum Scoparium (South Sea Myrtle) (E). Although half-hardy, it will do in a sheltered garden, or against a warm wall. It bears white hawthorn-like flowers of great fragrance in spring, and reaches about 8 ft. It likes equal parts of peat, loam and sand, and protection if the winter is hard. It is a very elegant, charming shrub, and one that I definitely recommend.

Prune: very lightly in spring.

Propagate: cuttings in autumn.

Linnæa borealis (Twin Flower) (E). This is a most glorious scented and attractive trailing shrub, which is good for rockeries and banks. It has pink and white bell-shaped flowers in May and June. It likes a certain amount of moisture, and thrives in woodlands in a mixture of sand and peat.

Prune: not necessary.

Propagate: division in October or March.

Lippia citriodora (Sweet-scented Verbena, Herb Louisa) (D). This half-hardy climber has lilac flowers with a fresh lemon scent. (Syn. *Aloysia citriodora.*) It does best against a warm south wall which is sheltered. It flowers in August, grows 10 to 15 ft., and is not fussy about soil.

Prune: cut to within one inch of the base in February.

Propagate: cuttings in March in the greenhouse.

Liquidambar (Sweet Gum Tree) (D). These hardy trees have deliciously fragrant leaves, with small greenish-yellow flowers in spring. *L. styraciflua* can attain 50 ft., but is unlikely to do so in this country. They are very slow growing, and one I had only reached four and a half feet after five years. They are useful in shrubberies in a deep moist loam.

Prune: shape if necessary in November.

Propagate: layering in spring.

Liriodendron tulipfera (Tulip Tree) (D). A very beautiful cousin of the magnolia, the Tulip Tree has bright glossy leaves, and very fragrant yellow flowers in August. Unfortunately it does not flower until it is very old, and is not much use to the gardener who has only a small amount of space available, and who wants blooms within a reasonable time. Although hardy, it should have a sheltered place, in deep rich soil, where it may reach 50 ft.

Prune: lightly to keep shape.

Propagate: layering in spring.

Lonicera (Honeysuckle) (D and E). There are so many that it is difficult to make a choice, but one of the best is the old-fashioned *L. Periclymenum* (the Common Honeysuckle) which has heavily scented flowers, red and yellow, in June, and which sometimes last until September. It grows 10 to 20 ft., depending upon what nourishment it can find at its feet. *L. sempervirens* (Evergreen Honeysuckle) has lovely scarlet and yellow blooms from May to August, and grows 10 to 15 ft. It is not hardy enough for the Midlands or North of England. *L. japonica* is one of the most fragrant of the evergreens, with red and cream flowers, well scented, blooming from July to September, reaching 8 ft. Of the deciduous, *L. etrusca* is a beautiful purple and yellow in May, about 8 ft., and *L. Caprifolium* (Goat Leaf Honeysuckle) is a bright, clear yellow, and very free growing. It will soon smother a cottage wall, is not a bit particular about soil, and likes chalk. *L. tragophylla* is a warm orange-yellow from June to September, growing 10 to 20 ft., and being extremely fragrant. Another with an excellent scent is *L. fragrantissima*, a shrubby type, which is half-evergreen, grows 6 ft., and bears its creamy blooms from December to March. The deciduous kind will do anywhere, but the evergreens to best against south or west walls. They all like a rich ordinary soil.

Prune: *L. fragrantissima* lightly after flowering. The shrubby species should have from December to early spring the old wood cut out, and others should have the shoots of the previous year's growth to within about three inches of the base.

Propagate: layering August-November; cuttings September.

Magnolia (Cucumber Tree, Yulan) (D and E). Of all beautiful shrubs, there are few to compare with the magnolia for form and fragrance, and it is surprising that they are not found in every garden, for they are hardy, no trouble, and no more expensive than other shrubs. Of the deciduous species, *M. conspicua* (Yulan) is a white beauty, but flowering in early spring, may need protection, or should be grown in a sheltered position. It will grow as tall as 30 ft., but of course, will take a considerable time to do this. *M. acuminata* (The Cucumber Tree) with pale green and yellow blooms in May, *M. Fraseri*, a deep ivory with an incomparable scent in May, and *M. tripetala* (syn. *M. Umbrella*) a pure shining white of heavy fragrance, also in May, are some of the loveliest. Of the evergreens, *M. grandiflora*, a beautiful pure white, bears its strongly scented

49

flowers from July to August, and *M. glauca* (Swamp Bay) is an old ivory, very fragrant indeed, in June. This latter should really be termed half-evergreen, and like the others may need protection in a very severe winter. They all grow from 15 to 30 ft. high. They like a deep sandy loam in a sheltered position.

Prune: if necessary, the evergreens in spring, the deciduous after flowering.

Propagation: layering summer or autumn.

Myrica (Candelberry Myrtle) (D). *M. cerifera*, sometimes called the Wax Myrtle, has slim brownish leaves, and reaches 15 ft. *Gale* (Sweet Gale, or Bog Myrtle) grows about 4 ft. with brownish-green leaves. It is rarely seen in gardens, but is common in bogs. It is an unassuming, compact little shrub, with a very sharp fragrance. Quite hardy, they like moist shady positions in a sandy peat soil.

Prune: not necessary.

Propagate: cuttings in autumn or layering.

Myrtus (Myrtle) (E). The myrtles are half-hardy, needing a sheltered position and protection in winter. There are several species, all with white, very fragrant flowers in summer. They like an ordinary well-drained soil, with the protection of walls, and are too tender for the North or Midlands.

Prune: not necessary.

Propagate: cuttings summer and autumn.

Olea europæa (Wild Olive) (E). These half-hardy shrubs need sheltered positions, but are worth a little trouble and cosseting. They bear white blooms of great fragrance in summer, and will grow up to 20 ft. They like shelter, sun, and sandy loam. They do well against walls.

Prune: slightly in April if necessary.

Propagate: cuttings in greenhouse in summer.

Olearia Haastii (New Zealand Daisy Bush or Victorian Snow Bush) (E). This is a nice bushy little shrub about

5 ft., covered in summer with a wealth of white starry flowers. The leaves have an attractive musky scent. They like a sandy loam in a sunny border. They have been known to grow very high, but this takes many years. They are half-hardy.

Prune: not necessary.

Propagate: cuttings in summer.

Osmanthus (Fragrant Olive) (E). *O. Delavayi* is white and strongly scented, flowering in April, 5 to 8 ft. high. It likes shelter, sun, and a loamy soil.

Prune: trim is necessary in April.

Propagate: cuttings in summer.

Philadelphus (Syringa, Mock Orange) (D). These easily grown, hardy shrubs are very beautiful, and of exquisite perfume. *P. coronarius* (Mock Orange) is a cloud of pearl-white in June, growing 10 ft. *P. Delavayi* is a pure white, with a very heavy scent in June, from 6 to 10 ft. It is difficult to make a choice, for all are beautiful, and all wonderfully scented. They like ordinary soil and sun.

Prune: thin out old shoots, and prune lightly after flowering.

Propagate: suckers or layering in spring.

Phillyrea (Jasmine Box, Mock Privet) (E). All the *Phillyreas* are hardy and useful for planting under trees for they do not mind damp and drips. *P. decora* has by far the best scent from its little white flowering in May, smelling like hawthorn. It does in ordinary soil and sun or shade.

Prune: straggly shoots in spring.

Propagate: cuttings in autumn.

Photinia (Chinese Hawthorn or Eriobotrya) (E). *P. serrulata* is white in May, and half-hardy. It grows about 10 ft., and likes light deep soil and sun.

Prune: April.

Propagate: cuttings in August.

Prunus (Common Almond, Myrobalan Plum, Double

Cherry, Japanese Apricot, etc.) (D). There is such a very large number of beautiful species that it is best to consult a nurseryman, and if possible, to see them in bloom before buying.

Raphiolepis (Incian Hawthorn) (E). The hardy *R. japonica* has the most fragrant white blossoms in June, and grows 10 ft. The half-hardy *R. indica* (Indian Hawthorn) with its pink-tinged flowers in midsummer is attractive. They do best in equal parts of peat, loam and silver sand, in the shelter of a south wall.

Prune: lightly to keep a good shape.

Propagate: cuttings in autumn.

Rhododendron. Formerly Azaleas and Rhododendrons were classed separately, but they are now classed under one heading. There is such an enormous number that it is best to consult a nurseryman, and to see them in bloom. Of the true rhododendrons, *R. calophytum*, rosy-white, is very fragrant, and of the azaleas, *A. occintale*, white and yellow, is very well scented. The azaleas are well worth a place in the garden, not only for their wonderful range of vivid colours, but for the delightful honey-scent which most of them possess. They prefer peat and leaf mould, but will grow in ordinary soil so long as it is not lime or chalk. They need plenty of water in dry weather, and a mulch of well-rotted manure in winter is most beneficial.

Prune: rhododendrons only need slight pruning to keep a good shape, and the dead blooms removed. Azaleas need no pruning, except to remove old or weak and straggly wood, and dead blooms removed.

Propagate: all can be increased by cuttings in late summer or layering in early spring.

Ribes aureum (Buffalo Currant) (D). This has yellow jasmine-like flowers with a delicate scent, quite unlike the strong, acrid unpleasant smell of the ordinary pink flowering currant. It flowers in April, in ordinary soil, and likes sun. Grows about 6 to 8 ft., and is absolutely hardy.

Prune: after flowering.

Propagate: cuttings late autumn to February.

Rosa (Rose) (D). Roses are not often considered as shrubs, but there are a number which are really flowering shrubs, and unsuitable in a rose garden or border, but far more in place in a shrubbery or edge of a wild garden. Some of the old-fashioned ones, alas so rarely seen now, are most beautiful, and surpass all the modern "lovelies" for fragrance. It is a pity they are not in every garden. They should be. Space should be made for them, even in a tiny garden.

R. rubrifolia bears glorious deep red blooms from June to August. It has deep red foliage and stems, is a very vigorous grower, reaches 5 to 7 ft., and needs fairly hard pruning.

R. centifolia muscosa (Moss Rose). This beautiful old rose has the most perfect scent. The old-fashioned rosy-pink blooms last well and appear in July. Perpetual White, and the two pinks Common Moss and Crested Moss, are also lovely, very fragrant and vigorous. They need practically no pruning, but should not be allowed to become too large and untidy.

R. rugosa (Japanese Rose). A lovely purple red, flowering from June to September, reaching 6 ft.

R. centifolia (Cabbage Rose). Has perhaps the most wonderful scent of all. Rosy-purple flowers in June. 6 ft.

R. centifolia provincialis (Provence Rose). Rosy pink with a similar scent to the Cabbage Rose. Blooms in June. 4 to 5 ft.

R. Moyesii. A dark red velvety beauty, rich in scent and colour. Flowers June to July. 6 to 8 ft.

R. lutea (Austrian Briar). A bright yellow followed by black hips. Flowers in June, about 4 ft., and has extremely lovely stems which are very shiny.

R. damascena (Damask Rose). White to red. The York

and Lancaster rose. Very fragrant, flowering in June. 4 to 6 ft.

R. Muschata (Musk Rose). Large clusters of creamy white single blooms. Grows 15 to 30 ft. high, very vigorously, and does well to cover a pergola or summer house. The hybrid musks are all charming, and no trouble. They have rather attractive narrow, blue green leaves. No pruning necessary, only cut out old dead wood.

R. gallica (Rosa Mundi). Its rich dark red blooms have such a wonderful scent as to be indescribable. It blooms June to July, is a very vigorous grower, has beautiful thick dark leaves, and reaches about 4 ft.

R. rubiginosa (Sweet Briar). These roses make lovely hedges. On a June evening, especially after rain, the air is heavily scented with their sweetness. The Penzance Briars are delightful, but have not quite such a powerful scent. Of these, Flora McIvor, blush-white, Anne of Gierstein, deep crimson, and Lady Penzance, coppery yellow, all make lovely hedges or, of course, can be grown separately. They still remain attractive in autumn with their brilliant fruits. The Sweet Briar proper should not be allowed to grow more than 4 to 5 ft., but the Penzance Briars can go up to 10 ft. when necessary.

One attraction of all these roses mentioned is that they need so little attention. They are best allowed to grow at will, with just the old wood thinned out occasionally to make room for new growth. Do not clip rose hedges, just prune out the old dead wood. Cut out also branches pointing into the centre, so that it does not become congested.

Rosmarinus officinalis (Rosemary) (E). This old-fashioned shrub cannot be omitted from any garden, with its sweetly fragrant leaves, and flowers of lilac hue. It makes a beautiful background for more colourful plants,

and is beloved by bees. It thrives in ordinary soil and
sunshine, and blooms from February to April.

Prune: not necessary.

Propagate: cuttings in spring and summer.

Rubus (Raspberry, Bramble, etc.) (D). *R. odoratus* (the
Virginian Raspberry) is the most fragrant, with purple-red
blooms in summer, reaching 6 ft. *R. nutkanus* has white
flowers in summer. It is called the Nootka Sound Bramble,
and reaches the same height. *R. spectabilis* (The Salmon
Berry) is a lovely rosy red in summer, and is also about
6 ft. They are useful for sun or shade, particularly in
shrubberies, or at the back of borders. They do in
ordinary soil.

Prune: cut away old shoots after flowering.

Propagate: division in autumn.

Skimmia japonica (E). The white flowers in spring are
very strongly scented, and in autumn the berries are a
beautiful scarlet. The male and female flowers are borne
on separate plants. They are quite hardy, grow 3 to 4 ft.,
like loam and peat and part shade.

Prune: not necessary.

Propagate: layering in autumn.

Solanum crispum. A fragrant blue-purple, very fast
growing climber. The little flowers are rather like the
potato, of which, of course, it is a near relation, if a very
superior one. It blooms in June, grows about 20 ft. and
likes good loam and leaf mould. Needs a warm, sheltered
position.

Prune: cut out weak growth in spring.

Propagate: cuttings in late spring.

Spartium junceum (Yellow Spanish Broom) (D). This is
a most valuable shrub, for it will grow anywhere, and is a
picture of burnished bright gold in summer, from 6 to 9 ft.
high. It has a warm honey scent.

Prune: not necessary.

Propagate: seeds in spring or autumn.

Styrax japonicum (D). The waxen snowdrop-like flowers have a sweet perfume in July. It is quite hardy, enjoying a sunny border, or warm south wall, and growing from 10 to 25 ft. It is rather similar to the Snowdrop Tree. A light peaty soil is best for it.

Prune: not necessary.

Propagate: layering spring or autumn.

Syringa (Lilac) (D). There are so many beautiful lilacs that it is advisable to consult a nurseryman's list, or to see them in bloom. *S. chinensis* (Rouen Lilac) bears deep violet flowers in May, grows 10 to 15 ft. *S. Josikæa* (Hungarian Lilac) is a deep blue-purple, also in May, and grows 10 to 12 ft. It is happy in any ordinary soil and sunshine.

Prune: very moderately, and be careful not to allow suckers to shoot up from the roots.

Propagate: suckers from October to early spring, cuttings August.

Ulex (Furze, Gorse, Whin) (E). The heavy honey scent of gorse is almost unequalled, and if the garden be large enough, a bush or two should be included. They will grow anywhere, sun or shade, rockery or woodland, or as a hedge. There is an old country saying that the only time a lad may not kiss his lass is when there is no flower to be found on the gorse. It is strange, but it is very rare to find gorse with no flower at all! *U. nanus* is a glittering gold in September, grows 2 ft. of more. *U. europæus florepleno* has double golden flowers in spring, about 5 to 6 ft.

Prune: not necessary, unless for a hedge, when trim in April.

Propagate: cuttings in August.

Viburnum (Guelder Rose, Snowball Tree) (D). Of the many beautiful and attractive viburnums, the most fragrant are the deciduous *V. bitchuense*, with white blossoms from May to July, growing 6 to 10 ft. *V. Carlesii*, pinkish white in April, 3 to 4 ft., and *V. fragrans*, blush-white in autumn, 10 ft. They are rather slow growing, and like a rich moist loam, in an open sunny position. These all have a most delicious fragrance, difficult to describe.

Prune: just keep trimmed and free from old wood.

Propagate: layering in autumn.

Wistaria (Grape Flower Vine, Kidney Bean Tree) (D). The fragrance of wistaria is a good a reason for having it against the house, as for its colour and form. The beautiful and vigorous climber *W. frutescens* (American Kidney Bean Tree) has lovely dark violet flowers from June to August, while *W. sinensis* (The Chinese Kidney Bean Tree) is a beautiful mauve in May. They are hardy, easy to grow, and not fussy about soil. They seem to do best against a south or west wall.

Prune: shorten any shoots not needed to within one inch of base.

Propagate: layering spring and autumn.

CLIMBERS AND WALL SHRUBS

CHAPTER FIVE

CLIMBERS AND WALL SHRUBS

CLIMBERS and wall shrubs play a very important part in the plan of the garden. Quite how important is not always realised, for how often does one see quite a charming garden surrounding a plain little house, which stands there positively blushing at its nakedness.

How often one sees really ugly houses which could so easily be camouflaged by the wise use of climbers.

I know a village, beautiful with thatched roofs and walls washed cream and pink, where someone chose to build a scarlet monstrosity of a bungalow. It was the talk of the neighbourhood, until someone gave the owner a *Polygonum baldschuanicum* or, to give it a prettier name, Knot Weed, and a rose. The Knot Weed leapt upon the bungalow, and threw a cascade of foamy white flowers across the roof, while the rose took a more sober course across the front door and round a window. In a short time that little place was transformed, and its ugliness almost completely hidden. Today it stands clothed magnificently by climbers and evergreen wall shrubs, and blends happily with the landscape.

One of the blessings of climbers is that they take up so little space, which is an important factor in a small garden. Also, if they are well planted at first, they need little more attention. But planting is important. The soil should be dug a good three feet deep and the same width, and if it is not particularly rich, it should be replaced by some good leaf mould, loam and well-rotted manure. If the soil is good, just mix manure with it. If you are planting something which likes peat, it is a good idea to make up a good bed of peat and manure for it. This little extra trouble at first will be well repaid in later years.

Once again, I must stress the importance of shrubs against the house, for it is they which form the essential link between house and garden.

CLIMBERS AND WALL SHRUBS

Abelia trifloral. This does best against south walls. See also "Fragrant."

Actinidia polygama. Is a good climber for walls, trellis, tree stumps, etc. See also "Fragrant."

Akebia quinata. A most attractive twiner needing trellis to support it against a south wall for preference. See also "Fragrant."

Aristolochia (Birthwort, Dutchman's Pipe) (D). *A. sipho*, called the Dutchman's Pipe on account of its quaint pipe-like shape, has browny-purple and yellow blooms in May, and grows from 15 to 30 ft. *A. tomentosa* is purple with very large leaves, flowers in July, and grows 10 to 15 ft. These hardy climbers are inclined to be rampant, and need only ordinary well-drained soil, in almost any position.

Prune: not necessary.

Propagate: cuttings in greenhouse in summer.

Azara dentata. Best against a south wall. See also "Fragrant".

Berberidopsis corallina (Coral Berry) (E). Lovely pendant clusters of crimson flowers adorn this shrub in summer. They are well set off by dark green leaves which are glaucous underneath. Growing 8 ft., it is hardy in the south, but is best treated as half-hardy in the north. Should be placed against a south or west wall.

Prune: straggly shoots in April.

Propagate: layering in autumn.

Berberis (E and D).   These make excellent wall shrubs. *B. aquifolium* (syn. *Mahonia aquifolium*) is very useful for a north wall.   It is yellow flowered in April, and later in the year it has dark berries with a beautiful violet bloom on them.   It is an evergreen, and grows about 6 ft.   A deciduous worth having against the house is *B. polyantha*, for it has graceful arching stems, scarlet berries, and fiery coloured foliage in autumn.   The blooms are yellow in June, it reaches 8 ft., and in undoubtedly one of the best. See also "Fragrant" and "Dwarfs."

Berchemia (Supple Jack) (D).   These hardy climbers like to be against a south wall in well-drained sandy loam.   *B. flavescens* is white in July, reaches 10 ft., while *B. racemosa* is greenish-white in September, about 8 ft.

Prune: remove old and weak wood early spring.

Propagate: cuttings in autumn.

Bignonia capreolata (Cross Vine, Trumpet Flower) (D). This is a glorious scarlet in summer, growing 10 to 15 ft., being quite hardy and happy in ordinary soil, although peat is its preference.   It does best against a south wall, but will do in other positions.   They are relations of the *Tecoma*, but the scarlet is less orangy than the former.   They might be found a little delicate in the north, and should be put in a sheltered place there.

Prune: just prune away a proportion of the weak shoots in spring.

Propagate: cuttings in spring in the greenhouse.

Billardiera longiflora (Blue Apple Berry) (E).   It is not wise to attempt to grow the *Billardias* unless in really mild districts, and then they must be against a sheltered south wall.   The flowers are creamy white to purple in summer and are succeeded by blue berries in autumn.   It reaches 15 ft.

Prune: cut away weak shoots in April.

Propagate: cuttings in greenhouse.

Calycanthus. Useful for any wall. See also "Fragrant."

Carpentaria. Preferably a south wall. See also "Fragrant."

Ceanothus. This is not really a climber, but is usually treated as one, and is one of the best for walls. The two following evergreens are useful:—*C. rigidus*, with glorious violet-blue flowers from March to May, growing 15 to 20 ft., and *C. Veitchianus*, a delicate powder blue in May, about 10 ft. Although deciduous, Gloire de Versailles cannot be omitted, for its lavender-blue flowers in July, about 10 ft. See also "Fragrant."

Celastrus scandens (Staff Vine, Climbing Bitter-Sweet) (D). The yellow flowers in summer are followed by very attractive orange and scarlet seeds. This is very hardy and useful, doing well in shade where other things refuse to grow, and not objecting to a north or north-east wall. Thrives in ordinary soil, grows about 20 ft.

Prune: cut off weak shoots and tips of main shoots early spring.

Propagate: layering autumn or spring.

Chimonanthus. Not a very tall grower, but good against south or west walls. See also "Fragrant."

Clematis. Of this large and beautiful family, I would particularly recommend the following, having greatly enjoyed the company of them all:—*C. vitalba* (Traveller's Joy), a deciduous, with white blossoms in July, should be more often seen, for it is a very quick grower, and most useful to cover an unsightly wall, shed, or summer house. *C. armandi*, an evergreen with ivory-white blooms in April, will reach as much as 30 ft., and has beautiful dark leaves. *C. montana*, a deciduous with white blooms in May, from 15 to 25 ft., is a very vigorous, almost rampant chap, and looks particularly attractive climbing against an evergreen tree, when its blooms have the appearance of a white cloud.

C. jackmani, the old-fashioned, deciduous, takes a lot of beating, and I find it does better by not pruning too hard. *Vitalba* should be allowed to grow at will, while *armandi*, *flammula* and *montana* should just have old growth removed to keep them neat, and *jackmani* must be cut back in February.   See also ''Fragrant.''

Cotoneaster (Rockspray, Rose Box) (E and D).   The *Cotoneasters* are among the best of wall shrubs, their attractively shaped branches clothe a wall with a neat grace.   They are one of the first things I would plant against a wall, and they are most accommodating, objecting neither to soil, position, shade nor sun, and not minding chalk.   *C. huxifolia*, an evergreen with white flowers in April, has bright red berries throughout the winter, and reaches 12 ft.   *C. acuminata*, a deciduous, is pale pink in April, later red berries, grows about the same height.

Prune: unnecessary.

Propagate: cuttings in autumn, layering spring.

Crataegus.   See ''Fragrant.''

Cydonia (Quince) (D).   While the quinces are often grown as standards, I prefer them as wall shrubs, trained fan-shaped, so that both flowers and fruits are shown to better advantage,   Blooming before the leaves appear, they have a rather wax-like, charmingly artificial appearance. *C. cathayensis* has white blooms in early summer, grows 8 ft.   *C. japonica* has mellow-brick red flowers about April or May, grows the same height.   They enjoy any ordinary soil.

Prune: shorten the side growths to four leaves in summer, allowing the extremity of each branch to grow.

Propagate: cuttings in autumn.

Forsythia.   Does well against south or west walls.   See also ''Fragrant.''

Garrya elliptica (E).   Usually grown as a wall shrub, and useful as it does not mind north walls.   It is hardy and bears long greenish-yellow catkins from March to May. Sometimes they are from 9 inches to 1 foot long, and are most attractive. It is a shrub not often seen, and it should be, for not only is it most useful as an evergreen, but it has great character.

Prune: not necessary.

Propagate: cuttings in autumn.

Hibiscus syriacus (Rose of Sharon, Syrian Mallow, Shrubby Althæa) (D). Syn. *Althæa frutex*. This makes a lovely wall shrub, growing 10 to 12 ft., preferring sunshine and a rich loam. There are several varieties of this species, all about the same height, with funnel-shaped blooms in autumn, single and double, in various colours such as white, pink and crimson. They flower from August to October. *H. syriacus* is perhaps one of the most attractive, the flowers being a purplish colour, with crimson blotches. They are showy things, and demand no particular attention or soil. They will even do quite well in shade.

Prune: not necessary, just cut out dead wood after flowering.

Propagate: cuttings in autumn.

Humulus Lupulus (Common Hop). Although, strictly speaking, this is a perennial, it is such a useful climber that it must be included. It is indispensable if one wants to clothe a wall or hut quickly. It is attractive and fast growing. It likes a deep well-manured soil, and is excellent to cover trellis or tree stumps, as well as walls. The pretty little green female flower (the hop) is ready to gather in September if wished. The plants do better if top-dressed each spring with well-rotted manure.

Prune: cut down plants in October.

Propagate: division in March.

Hydrangea petiolaris (D). This is an unusual and most attractive climber for a west wall. In a fairly short time it will quite cover a large space, and has lovely white flower

64

heads, sometimes ten inches across. It is self-clinging, blooms in June, and will do well in an ordinary well-drained soil.

Prune: not necessary, except to remove dead wood.

Propagate: cuttings in cold frame in August.

Jasminum. *J. revolutum* is a particularly good yellow, and a quick and vigorous grower. See also "Fragrant."

Kerria japonica (Jew's Mallow) (D). This is a good shrub for a south or west wall. It has single orange-yellow flowers in May, lasting until June, and reaches up to 8 ft. It is quite hardy, thriving in ordinary soil. It is an old-fashioned beauty, with its straight, slender stems, and should be seen more often.

Prune: cut out old wood in May.

Propagate: cuttings in summer, or division.

Lippia citriodora. See also "Fragrant."

Lonicera. See also "Fragrant."

Lycium (Box Thorn, African Tea Tree, Duke of Argyll's Tea Tree) (D). These shrubs are often seen in old-fashioned cottage gardens, and are useful as climbers or hedges. *L. afrum* has violet and crimson flowers in June and grows about 8 ft. *L. sinense* (syn. *L. barbarum*), the Box Thorn, or Duke of Argyll's tea-tree, as it is sometimes called, is purple and yellow in summer, about 10 ft., with scarlet berries in autumn. They are quite hardy, and will do in any soil.

Prune: remove weak growths in autumn.

Propagate: cuttings in autumn.

Magnolia. Of this exquisite family, there are many beauties eminently suitable for walls. See also "Fragrant."

Menispermum canadense (Moon Seed, Moon Creeper) (D). This climber will do well in ordinary rich soil, preferably in a damp, shady place, where it will produce a wealth of yellow flowers in summer. It grows about 10 ft., and is hardy.

C

Prune: cut out weak shoots in autumn or early spring.

Propagate: cuttings in spring.

Mutisia decurrens (D). This climber is often grown in a cold greenhouse, and perhaps because of that people imagine it to be delicate, but indeed that is not so ; it is quite hardy, and will grow in ordinary soil, with a little shelter and shade. Slugs are very fond of it in spring and the roots should be protected from them. Keep well watered in dry weather. It has orange-yellow flowers in summer and grows 6 ft.

Prune: very lightly after flowering.

Propagate: cuttings in spring.

Myrtus. See also "Fragrant."

Passiflora (Passion Flower) (D). This is a most unusual and exceedingly beautiful climber, and I do not know why it is not seen more often, for although it is half-hardy, providing the district is reasonably mild, and it is against a south or south-west wall, it does very well and is no trouble at all. *P. cœrulea* is white, blue and purple in summer, and will reach 20 ft. It needs plenty of water in dry weather, and regular feeding with liquid manure during summer makes a great deal of difference to the blooms. The fruits in late autumn are large, egg-shaped, and golden. Ordinary soil is suitable.

Prune: very, very lightly in February, just tipping the shoots.

Propagate: layering in summer.

Periploca græca (Silk Vine) (D). This hardy twiner is useful for walls, sheds and trellis, for it will do in any position, and in ordinary soil. It has green and brown flowers in July, grows 20 to 30 ft., and during the flowering season, applications of liquid manure are a help.

Prune: not necessary.

Propagate: layering autumn.

Phlomis Fruticosa (Jerusalem Sage) (E). These shrubs

are useful for a house wall, preferably south or west. They are hardy, enjoy ordinary soil and sun, and grow about 4 ft. They have downy stems, and golden yellow flowers in June.

Prune: not necessary.

Propagate: cuttings in August.

Piptanthus nepalensis (Nepal Laburnum) (E). This, like the preceding shrub, is better grown against a wall, and this is particularly good against a summer-house or garage. It is quite hardy, has bright yellow flowers in May, and grows between 8 to 10 ft. high. It does better in a rich soil, and if in the North or Midlands of England, it should have the protection of a south wall.

Prune: just tidy straggly shoots after flowering.

Propagate: cuttings in autumn.

Polygonum baldschaunicum (Knot Weed) (D). This rampant, vigorous shrubby climber with the most forceful personality is indeed a treasure for some positions, but needs planting with discretion, for it would certainly be too rampant for some positions. If you wish to clothe a summer-house, or cover a trellis to shut out the next door garden, then this is the one, for it will do the job, and do it quickly. The only disadvantage is that it is deciduous, but even when it has lost its leaves in winter, there still remain many twisting, twining brown branches as a thin covering, until the spring. In summer, it throws a cascade of creamy foamy flowers over everything, until late autumn. It will grow anywhere, and does not mind poor dry soil.

Prune: cut it back as often as it becomes too spreading.

Propagate: division of roots in autumn.

Pyracantha (Firethorn) (E). This is not really a climber but is usually treated as one, as it is shown off to far better advantage if trained against a wall. *P. angustifolia* has white flowers in May, later orange-yellow berries, and grows about 10 ft. *P. crenulata* is also white in June, with orange berries, and grows the same height. They are hardy, will grow in ordinary soil, and will do in most positions.

Prune: lightly to keep a neat shape in early spring.

Propagate: cuttings in autumn.

Rapiolepis japonica. This often grows better as a wall shrub than in the open. See also ''Fragrant.''

Rhodotypos kerrioides (White Kerria) (D). This hardy cousin of the Kerria has pure white flowers in May about two inches across, and grows 5 ft. It is not often seen, but is charming and easy to grow, being happy in ordinary soil, and almost any position.

Prune: cut away old wood only in May.

Propagate: cuttings in autumn.

Rhus (Sumach, Wig Tree, Smoke Tree, Stag's-horn Sumach) (D). These most attractive and unusual shrubs can be grown against a wall or in the open. *R. Cotinus* (Smoke Tree, Wig Tree, or Venetian Sumach) has stalks covered with fine hairs, giving it a smoky appearance, with beautifully coloured crimson and yellow leaves in autumn, and in July, greyish flowers. Grows 8 ft. *R. glabra* (Smooth Sumach) has small fruits covered with little red hairs, greenish flowers in August, and also has lovely foliage in autumn. About 8 ft. They are certainly characters with their red, fluffy, wig-like appearance ; they are hardy, and happy in ordinary soil.

Prune: lightly after flowering.

Propagate: cuttings in autumn.

Robinia (False Acacia, Locust Tree, Rose Acacia) (D). The *Robinias* are hardy and easy to grow, the most attractive being *R. hispida* (Rose Acacia), a very pretty pink in May, about 9 ft. This does best against a south wall, for it likes sun.

Prune: just trim to keep shape.

Propagate: cuttings in autumn.

Rosa. A house without roses growing upon it is a house

incomplete. There are innumerable beauties suitable for walls, and a nurseryman's list should be consulted. I would certainly not omit Gloire de Dijon, for that old favourite takes a lot of beating with its beautiful salmon-yellow blooms and lovely scent. It is useful too, for it does not mind a north or east wall. Also Hugh Dickson, a gloriously scented deep crimson, which again does not object to a north or east outlook. See also "Fragrant."

Schizandra rubrifolia (D). A very handsome hardy climber with red blooms in May, lovely leaves, and, in autumn, red berries. It grows about 12 ft., and likes loam, peat, and sun.

Prune: trim straggly shoots in spring.

Propagate: cuttings in autumn.

Schizophragma hydrangeoides (Climbing Hydrangeas) (D). This self-clinging climber is hardy, but not enough to stand very cold districts. It likes a sunny wall in a sheltered spot. I have grown it in a very exposed position in the south, where it survived and flourished, but I think that was due to luck, and the fact that at the time I did not know it was on the tender side. It has old-ivory flowers in July, and will reach 25 to 30 ft. It is quite happy in ordinary soil, and requires no special attention.

Prune: just trim untidy shoots in spring.

Propagate: cuttings in spring.

Solanum jasminoides (Jasmine Nightshade). This half-hardy climbing perennial must be included in the list, for it is very attractive, and seems to improve with age. It has blue and white flowers in June, which sometimes last as long as October. It grows 15 ft., and should be placed against a warm south wall. I would not advise it for a northern or cold district. It likes peat and leaf mould for its feet. See also "Fragrant."

Prune: cut away weak growth in spring.

Propagate: cuttings in late spring, in a frame.

Tamarix (Tamarisk, Manna Plant) (E and D). Although these hardy shrubs are usually planted in shrubberies, they can sometimes be placed with advantage against a wall. They are hardy, thriving in ordinary soil, and doing particularly well by the sea. *T. anglica* (the Common Tamarisk) is pinky-white in August, an evergreen growing about 6 ft. *T. hispida* is pink also in August. This is a deciduous, about 4 ft., and does not like a wind-swept position. Their feathery flowers have rather an attractive misty look.

Prune: it is important to cut out straggly shoots in autumn and to keep the bush neat, otherwise the appearance can be absolutely spoilt.

Propagate: cuttings in autumn.

Tecoma (Trumpet Flower, Moreton Bay Trumpet-Jasmine) (E) This very handsome and hardy climber is very attractive trained over an old tree, or pergola, or against the south wall of a house. *T. grandiflora* (syn. *Bignonia grandiflora*) has tubular-shaped rich orangy-red flowers in August, and grows up to 20 ft. It likes peat and rich loam.

Prune: just tip the shoots in spring.

Propagate: cuttings or layering in spring.

Tropæolum speciosum (Flame Flower). This hardy perennial is a cousin of the Nasturtium, and a beautiful one, which, although herbaceous in character, will live for years, and improve with time. It likes a damp shady place for its roots, and is useful for a north wall. It has long slender sprays of glorious crimson flowers in summer, and later, bright blue seeds. It sends forth new shoots each year, and needs trellis for support. Grows about 10 ft., and prefers a peaty soil.

Prune: not necessary.

Propagate: division of roots.

Veronica Hulkeana (Speedwell) (E). This makes a very pretty wall shrub, in a position where one does not want anything too large, as it grows 4 to 5 ft., and seems to do better against a wall than in the open sometimes. It is a very soft lavender-blue in summer, and enjoys ordinary soil and sun.

Prune: keep trimmed in spring.

Propagate: cuttings in autumn.

Vitis (Grape Vine, Virginian Creeper) (D). There are a number of ornamental vines, all with very fine colouring, and easy to grow, for they like ordinary soil, and do not object to lime. *V. vitacea* (the Common Virginian Creeper) is well known with its lovely red-tinged foliage, which is so brilliant in autumn. *V. Henryana* has leaves of a rather velvety texture, coloured green, white and pink, and turning to crimson in autumn. *V. heterophylla* (the Turquoise Berry Vine) has blue berries. These are all useful for house walls but, like other deciduous climbers, one should remember to plant evergreens between them, so that the walls do not look bare in winter.

Prune: not necessary, except to cut out straggly shoots in winter.

Propagate: cuttings in autumn.

Wistaria. One of the most attractive climbers, and the only thing against it is that it is inclined to be a little slow growing. See also ''Fragrant.''

GREENAWAY SKETCHES.

DWARFS AND MINIATURES

CHAPTER SIX

DWARFS AND MINIATURES.

IN the following list I have included shrubs which range from tiny creepers, barely a couple of inches above the ground, to those which grow approximately four feet high. These shrubs are intended for the small or average-sized rock garden, for the front of borders, and in the mixed herbaceous border.

The ordinary rock garden rarely has enough shrubs, and it should be borne in mind that this is another part of the garden where shrubs play an important role. In the case of evergreens, they are particularly valuable for their welcome greenery in winter, and both evergreen and deciduous are important for the protection they afford more tender plants, and for the form they give to the whole.

The same may be said of dwarfs and miniatures in herbaceous borders, and in small borders where there is little space to spare. Even in a tiny garden, dwarfs may be grown, and they will make it far more attractive and interesting then if only annuals and perennials were planted.

DWARFS AND MINIATURES

Abies (Silver Fir) (E). The dwarf conifers are very necessary in the rock garden to form shelter for less hardy plants, and being indifferent as to soil and position. *A. balsamea hudsonia* is a charming little thing, about 2½ ft. high, rather spreading in habit, but very neat.

Prune: not necessary.

Propagation: by seeds in the greenhouse in spring.

73

D

Acer (Maple) (D. and semi-evergreen). The delightful little Japanese Maples take such a great number of years to grow to any height that they may be considered dwarfs. *A. Japonicum aureum* has leaves of a most brilliant scarlet and orange, while *A. palmatum dissectum* has the most delicate fern-like bronze foliage. They will grow in ordinary soil, and are quite easy, providing they are not in damp places, or exposed to cold east winds.

Prune: not necessary.

Propagate: layering in autumn.

Andromeda (Marsh Rosemary) (E). The delightful little *A. polifolia* rarely grows more than 1 ft. high, and its pale rose flowers in May are well set off by the grey foliage. It is not really necessary to plant it in a boggy place, but it does prefer damp peat, and a little sun. See also *Pieris*, *Cassandra*, *Leucothœ* and *Zenobia*, which were formerly included in this genus.

Prune: not necessary.

Propagate: layering in autumn.

Azalea. If the rock garden be large enough, an azalea here and there adds greatly to its attraction. They are also seen to advantage when planted mid-way in the herbaceous border. See under rhododendron in "Fragrant."

Berberis. The following are most suitable in rock gardens, or narrow borders:—The *Stenophylla* hybrids, *B. coccinea*, *B. gracillis compacta*, and *B. corallina*. The first has most brilliant buds and flowers, while *gracilis* is a miniature of great charm, and *corallina*, the tallest of the three, grows up to 3 ft., and has rich orange flowers and scarlet berries. All are evergreens. Of the deciduous, *B. Thunbergii minor* is low and spreading, with pale yellow flowers in April and red berries. *B. Wilsonæ* has pale gold flowers in summer, followed by coral berries. Both are about 3 ft. See also "Fragrant" and "Climbers."

Bruckenthalia spiculifolia (E). This is a heather-like

shrub, with pale pink flowers in summer, about 6 inches high. It likes sun and peat. If the garden is lacking in the latter, a hole should be dug and filled with peat, to get the best from this plant. It is charming in the rock garden.

Prune: not necessary.

Propagate: cuttings in spring.

Buddleia variabilis nanhœnsis (E). A dwarf edition of *B. v. magnifica*, which never grows more than 4 ft., and spreads about 3 ft. It has delightful deep lilac flowers in summer. It thrives in ordinary soil and sun. See also "Fragrant."

Calluna (Ling, Heather) (E). *C. vulgaris* is a hardy chap which enjoys peaty soil and plenty of sun. It is purple in spring and grows about 1 ft. high. *C. aurea* has very pretty golden foliage, flowers July to September, and also grows a foot. They like a damp boggy place if possible, with peat. The edge of a shady shrubbery is quite good for them.

Prune: not necessary.

Propagate: division in spring.

Cassandra (E). *C. calyculata* (syn. *Andromeda calyculata*), a member of the Erica family, has white flowers in spring, and grows up to 3 ft. It likes peat and leaf mould.

Prune: tidy straggly shoots after flowering.

Propagate: layering in autumn.

Cassinia (Golden Heath) (E). *C. fulvida* is hardy and beautiful, growing up about 3 ft., and happy in ordinary soil and sun. It covers itself in summer with clusters of small white flowers, and has attractive gold-tinted foliage.

Prune: not necessary.

Propagate: cuttings in summer.

Cassiope (E). *C. fastigiata* is another charming member of the heath family, and is sometimes called *Andromeda fastigiata*. Like all heaths, it will not grow in lime, and to do its best it must have sandy peat, and a moist shady position. It has white flowers in spring, rather like lily of the valley blooms. It is quite hardy and, providing it has the soil it likes, is no trouble.

Prune: not necessary.

Propagate: layering in autumn.

Cistus. *C. crispus* and *C. purpureus* are both suitable for a rock garden, growing about 2 ft. high. Both are extremely beautiful, and very showy with their great brilliant blooms. The former has purple flowers, and the latter a red-purple. Both bloom in summer. See also "Fragrant."

Cotoneaster. Two evergreens which must be in the rock garden are *C. humifusa*, which is excellent for draping over a rock or bank, and has white flowers in April; and *C. thymifolia*, with thyme-like leaves, and rosy-white flowers. Both grow about 18 inches. See also "Climbers."

Cupressus tetragona minima (Cypress) (E). Another small conifer which is suitable for the rock garden. It is not fussy about soil or position, and is quite hardy.

Prune: not necessary.

Propagate: cuttings in autumn.

Cytisus (Broom) (D). These very attractive cousins of the Genistas are hardy, easy to grow, and delightful in a rock garden. *C. Ardoinii* is a light bright gold in spring, about 6 inches high. *C. kewensis*, a fine hybrid, with creamy flowers also in spring, and trailing in habit. *C. Beani* is a glorious deep gold in spring, about 1 ft. high. They should not be allowed to grow unchecked and straggly, otherwise they will lose their beauty. See also "Fragrant."

Daboecia (Irish Heath, St. Dabeoc's Heath) (E). These hardy little creatures thrive almost anywhere, providing the soil is not limy. They all grow about a foot high, and prefer a partly shaded position. *D. polifolia alba* and *D. p. bicolour*. The former is white, and the latter purplish-red. They flower from June until September.

Prune: not necessary.

Propagate: layering in autumn.

Daphne (D and E). *D. cneorum* is sometimes a little more tender than the others, but is well worth a little trouble, for it is one of the best, with rosy-purple flowers in May, growing about 1 ft. high. It is evergreen, as are *D. Blagayana* and *D. petræa*. The former has ivory blossoms in March, about 6 inches high, and the latter has bright purply-pink blooms the same month. These are two beauties. See also ''Fragrant.''

Deutzia (Japanese Snow Flower) (D). Of these cousins of the mock orange, I prefer the dwarf *D. gracilis*, which has single white pink-tinged flowers in May and June. It is very graceful and light. Growing only about 2 ft., it is hardy, and will do in ordinary soil.

Prune: just keep trimmed to a neat shape.

Propagate: cuttings in autumn.

Dryas (Mountain Avens) (E). *D. Drummondi* is a hardy trailer, and likes a peat soil and a very damp position. It has yellow flowers in June, and grows only about 3 inches high. It is, of course, excellent for a rock garden.

Prune: not necessary.

Propagate: cuttings in autumn.

Empetrum (Black-berried Heath, Crake Berry, Crow Berry) (E). *E. nigrum* is hardy, has pink flowers in May, black berries in autumn, and grows about 9 inches high. It likes a damp, shady situation, and prefers peat.

Prune: not necessary.

Propagate: cuttings in early autumn.

Erica (Heath) (E). These beautiful and hardy plants are certainly an asset to the rock garden or the front of shrub borders. Hardly any of them will grow in lime, but they like a sand and peat soil and sun. *E. darleyensis* has red flowers in mid-winter, and grows 2 ft. high. *E. vagans* (The Cornish Heath) has pink blooms from July to September, and is about 1 ft. *E. ciliaris* (The Dorset Heath) is red in summer, 9 inches high. *E. tetralix* (Cross-leaved

Heath, or Bell Heather) is a lovely deep rose from July to September, about 9 inches.

Prune: no pruning necessary, except to keep a neat shape.

Propagate: cuttings in early autumn.

Erinacea (The Hedgehog Broom) (E). *E. pungens* is a pale blue in spring, a most attractive little plant, growing about 1 ft. high, and revelling in a sunny position in the rock garden and peat in the soil.

Prune: not necessary.

Propagate: cuttings in autumn.

Euonymus (Spindle Tree) (E and D). This well-known hardy shrub does not object to shade, thrives in ordinary soil, and is no trouble to grow. *E. radicans* is the tiniest of them all, being only a foot high. It is an evergreen. The Spindle Trees are said to harbour the eggs of aphis which destroy sugar beet and bean crops. They certainly always harbour many caterpillars, and should be watched for these pests.

Prune: not necessary.

Propagate: division in autumn.

Fuchsia (Lady's Ear Drops) (D). To show themselves at their best, the fuchsias need a deep rich soil, partly shaded, and are better if watered in summer with liquid manure instead of plain water. They may need protection in a bad winter, but if they are grown in a mild district, they should be hardy enough. *F. macrostemma* is scarlet and purple in July, and its variety pumila is scarlet. Both of them can be kept the size required by pruning. They look very charming in the rock garden or at the corners of herbaceous borders.

Prune: some people advise hard pruning, but I prefer to cut them just enough to keep the bushes neat.

Propagate: cuttings in late autumn or early spring.

Gaultheria (Creeping Winter Green, Shallon, Canada

Tea, Partridge Berry) (E). These very useful plants look very well growing among rhododendrons and azaleas, as they are all peat loving. They will grow in an ordinary lime-free soil, but do very much better in peat. They are hardy, and prefer a little shade and dampness. *G. procumbens* is a creeping kind, with white flowers in July and August. *G. nummularioides* has pink-tinged flowers in August, and is trailing.

Prune: not necessary.

Propagate: seeds in autumn.

Genista pilosa. This is the best one for a rock garden. It has yellow blooms in June, and grows from 1 to 2 ft. See also ''Fragrant.''

Hedysarum multijugum (French Honeysuckle) (D). This has reddish-purple flowers in June, and grows up to 4 ft. It is happy in ordinary soil and sunshine.

Prune: cut back in autumn.

Propagate: cuttings in autumn.

Hymenanthera crassifolia (Semi-evergreen). This is an attractive shrub, with bright yellow flowers rather resembling pansy blooms, in summer, and berries in autumn of a pearl white tint. It likes peat and leaf mould and a sunny position. This is another which is suitable for the border of a rhododendron and azalea bed or a rockery. It grows about 3 ft., and is hardy.

Prune: just keep tidy.

Propagate: cuttings in autumn.

Hypericum (St. John's Wort, Aaron's Beard, Rose of Sharon, Tutsan) (E). The secret of making this well-known shrub a mass of brilliant golden blooms is manure. So often it is pushed into some sunless place where nothing else will grow, and where it is left with no more attention, and where it nobly blooms. But if it is given stable manure, it will cover itself with blossom and double its beauty. *H. Moserianum* is about 15 inches high, and has bright gold

79

flowers with crimson-tipped stamens from July to August. It is one of those very accommodating creatures which puts up with any sort of treatment and grows anywhere, but which certainly repays one for a little care and kindness.

Prune: trim a little in spring.

Propagate: cuttings in autumn.

Juniperus sabina tamariscifolia (The Gin Tree, Juniper, Savin) (E). The beautiful blue-green foliage makes this one of the prettiest of conifers, and delightful in the rock garden. It is prostrate, and suitable therefore for a bank or draping over a rock. It will grow in ordinary soil, and is not fussy about anything.

Prune: not necessary.

Propagate: cuttings in autumn.

Ledum latifolium (Marsh Rosemary, Labrador Tree) (E). A hardy, useful shrub which will grow in sun or shade and ordinary soil, providing it is not lime. It will flourish its white, pink-tinged clusters of blossom during May, and grows about 2 ft.

Prune: not necessary.

Propagate: layering autumn.

Leiophyllum buxifolium (Sand Myrtle) (E). A member of the heath family, which greatly resembles the Ledums. It grows 12 to 18 inches high, has small bright leaves, and clusters of white flowers in May. It is hardy, and likes a peaty soil.

Prune: not necessary.

Propagate: layering in autumn.

Linnæa. This is very suitable for the rock garden. See also "Fragrant."

Mitchella repens (Chequer Berry, North American Partridge Berry, Deer Berry) (E). A tiny little creature which is too small for a border, but which is charming in the rock garden, although even there, care must be taken that it is not hidden by larger plants. It is hardy, likes peat and a little shade, grows 3 inches high and throws forth a trail of little white and purple flowers in summer, followed by tiny red berries.

Prune: not necessary.

Propagate: cuttings in autumn.

Muehienbeckia axillaris (Australian Ivy) (D). Another tiny thing, which although only an inch or two high, spreads rapidly. It is not absolutely hardy, and may need protection in winter if in an exposed position. It does not mind lime, and likes sun.

Prune: not necessary.

Propagate: cuttings in autumn.

Pernettya (Prickly Heath) (E). *P. mucronata* is a lovely hardy creature, growing up to 3 ft., with sharp pointed leaves, and white flowers in June followed by berries. It will grow in a moist shady place or in moderate sun. It is as well to plant in groups to ensure fertilisation. The berries are white, pink, purple or black. It prefers a peaty soil.

Prune: not necessary.

Propagate: layering in spring.

Philadelphus purpureo-maculatus. A hybrid with white flowers blotched with purple, growing 4 to 5 ft., and blooming in June. See also "Fragrant."

Phyllodoce (E). These dwarf relations of the Ericas are admirable for the rock garden. *P. Breweri* is a rosy purple in May, 9 inches high. *P. cærulea* is a blue-purple in June, also 9 inches. They do in ordinary soil, and preferably a damp position.

Prune: not necessary.

Propagate: cuttings in autumn.

Pieris floribunda (E). The white flowers in spring are rather similar to the flowers of the lily of the valley. It is hardy, grows about 3 to 4 ft. high, and will do in ordinary soil, but not in lime. A rockery or bog is the ideal place.

Prune: tidy straggly shoots after flowering.

Propagate: layering in autumn.

81

Picea (Spruce) (E). There are several nice dwarfs, but *P. excelsa clanbrassiliana* is one of the best, with neat light green thick foliage. It needs a dry position in sandy loam, and is no trouble to grow.

Prune: not necessary.

Propagate: cuttings in autumn.

Pinus silvestris beauvronensis (E). A miniature Scots pine of great charm, with beautiful blue-green foliage. It is quite hardy and will grow in any ordinary soil, and does not mind chalk.

Prune: not necessary.

Propagate: seeds in a frame in spring.

Potentilla (Cinquefoil) (E). *P. fruticosa* is a bright yellow beauty, 3 ft. high, flowering from July to August. *P. Vilmoriniana* has paler, creamy-yellow flowers and silvery foliage, in the same months, and is a nice slim shape. The same height. These do well in ordinary soil in the rock garden in sun or shade.

Prune: remove old and dead wood in autumn.

Propagate: cuttings in autumn.

Prunus Nana (Dwarf Almond) (D). A neat, lovely shrub, covered with rosy blossom in March, about 3½ ft. high. It likes ordinary soil and sunshine.

Prune: tidy after flowering and remove dead wood.

Propagate: cuttings in early autumn.

Rhododendron (E and D). *R. amœnum*, an evergreen, has purplish rose flowers in May, and is a very bright beauty, growing 2 to 4 ft. *R. yedœnse* (syn. *R. yodogawa*), also evergreen, has rosy-lavender blooms in May, about 4 to 5 ft. These were formerly classed as azaleas. There is a number of the true rhododendrons suitable for the rock garden. I would certainly include *R. hirsutum*, with rosy-pink blooms in June, growing only 2 to 3 ft. high, and *R. kamtschaticum*, a tiny thing about 9 inches high, and bright rose flowers in late spring. These are both hardy ever-greens. See also "Fragrant."

Rhodothamnus (Ground Cistus) (E). Relations of the Ericas, these shrubs are hardy, and will do in ordinary soil, but should not be allowed to become dry in hot weather and should be watered well. *R. chamæcistus* (syn. *Rhododendron chamæcistus*) grows only 9 inches high, and is covered with pink blooms in spring.

Prune: not necessary.

Propagate: division at planting time.

Rosa. There are a number of delightful little roses suitable for rock gardens and small borders. The baby Little Dorrit is a good one, being only 15 inches high, and an attractive salmon pink. A nurseryman's list should be consulted. See also "Fragrant" and "Climbers."

Rosemarinus officinalis prostrata (E). A miniature edition of the well-known Rosemary. A trailer with purple flowers in April. Will grow in any position and soil, and prefers sun. See also "Fragrant."

Spiræa (Meadow Sweet) (D). Among the many lovely *Spiræas* some of the smaller ones are charming. *S. bullata* is a deep rosy tint, about 15 inches high, flowering in July. *S. Douglasii* is pink in August, about 4 to 5 ft. *S. japonica* (syn. *S. callosa*) is covered with rosy blossom in June, and *S. Thunbergi* is creamy white in early spring. Both are between 4 to 5 ft. high. All are hardy and do well in moist loam and a semi-shady position.

Prune: not necessary, except to remove straggly shoots after flowering.

Propagate: cuttings in early autumn.

Thuya (Arbor Vitæ) (E). *T. occidentalis ellwangeriana*, a dwarf form of the American Arbor Vitæ is a hardy useful shrub. The leaves are small and attractive bright green, with a slight russet tinge. They will do in any soil and position.

Prune: not necessary, except to keep a neat shape.

Propagate: cuttings in autumn.

Ulex. The tiny *U. nana* is suitable for rockeries and narrow borders, growing only a foot high, and bearing a great load of golden blossom in September. It is a little Gorse with great charm. See also "Fragrant."

Veronica. There are many Veronicas suitable for rock gardens and small borders. One can plant so as to have colour from May to October. *V. Hectori* is a pale lilac and white in July, about 12 inches high. *V. Chathamica* is purple in summer, the same height. See also "Climbers."

Viburnum Davidii. This is a neat little shrub, evergreen, and with white blooms in June, followed by lovely deep blue fruits. It grows only 2 ft. high, and is excellent for small spaces or mixed in the herbaceous border. See also "Fragrant."

Vinca (Periwinkle) (E). There are several charming Periwinkles which might well be honoured with a place in any garden, even though they be somewhat humble plants. Some have variegated leaves, touched with gold or silver, and all have bright lilac-blue flowers. *V. minor* (The Lesser Periwinkle), a little trailer, is covered with flowers in summer. They are not a bit fussy about soil, and will grow anywhere, especially in shady places or under trees where other things refuse to thrive. The only objection they seem to have is having their abode moved. They like to stay put.

Prune: not necessary.

Propagate: cuttings in spring.

Zenobia (E). This is a rather larger member of the Erica family, *Z. speciosa* growing up to 4 ft., with white flowers in summer. It has a variety, *pulverulenta*, with attractive greyish blue foliage. They like a peaty soil and a moist sheltered place such as the border of a shrubbery.

Prune: not necessary.

Propagate: cuttings at the end of summer.

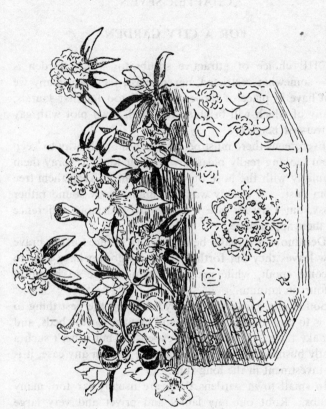

CHAPTER SEVEN

FOR A CITY GARDEN

CHAPTER SEVEN

FOR A CITY GARDEN

THE choice of attractive shrubs for a city garden is somewhat restricted, nevertheless, there are many we can have in place of those dreary all too familiar laurels, many of which will brighten the small town plot with gay flowers or berries.

Evergreens there must be, although the only way to keep them looking really pleased with their lot is to spray them regularly with the hose or watering can, to keep them free from dust. A weekly wash in summer may sound rather fussy, but I assure you it makes an enormous difference to their appearance.

Deciduous are really better for city grime, for the brave new leaves they put forth each spring do not have time to become spoilt, while many of them change to beautiful colours in autumn.

Soil in city gardens is usually sour, and the best thing to do is to buy some good loam and manure for the beds, and remake them. It may sound expensive, but it isn't such a costly business as one would suppose and, in any case, it is an investment in the long run.

In small town gardens there are usually far too many shrubs. Root out any laurel and privet and very large trees, and replace them with a few choice shrubs and climbers. None will do well if overcrowded and hungry. Never plant large trees, or they will make the house dark and gloomy eventually, and will eat all the goodness in the soil. Things such as Chestnuts, Limes and Plane Trees should never be put in a small garden. There is no lovelier tree for a city garden than the Silver Birch. It is beautiful at all seasons, and eats only moderately.

A few years ago I saw a charming little garden in Chelsea, with paved paths, and borders filled with rhododendrons all in full bloom. The great bunches of pink bloom made a most surprising and charming sight in the grey street.

If you live in a town, try some of the gayer shrubs. Given a little care and extra kindness, there's no reason at all why they should'nt "do!"

FOR A CITY GARDEN

Ailantus (Tree of Heaven, Tree of the Gods (D). This hardy and very handsome tree has only one fault, it is rather on the large size for the average town garden. *A. glandulosa* has white flowers, and the foliage is rather attractive. It might be useful in a reasonably large garden, especially if kept trimmed to the shape required, otherwise it is liable to grow about 30 ft. high. It does in an ordinary soil, and preferably a moist position. The best thing to do is to cut it back hard every year.

Prune: as mentioned.

Propagate: pot up bits of the roots.

Amelanchier (Grape-pear, Snowy Mespilus, June Berry) (D). The *Amelanchiers* are hardy, and will grow almost anywhere. In spring they are a white cloud of blossom, and in autumn the leaves are painted and burnished yellow, crimson and orange, so that the shrubs are almost as beautiful then as in their white spring gowns. *A. alnifolia* and *A. oblongifolia*, both white in April, are two of the best for small places, for they rarely grow more than 8 to 10 ft. high and, in any case, are very slow growing. They are content in ordinary soil, and are shrubs of great beauty, worthy of a place in any garden, town or country.

Prune: lightly after flowering.

Propagate: cuttings in autumn.

Buxus (Box) (E). The little Box-trees are useful, hardy, and have an old-world charm. They will thrive in any soil, in sun or in shade. They can be allowed to grow as little specimen bushes, and will reach about 6 ft. high in time, although they are slow growing, or they can be used as edgings, and clipped. *B. suffruticosa* is the best for edgings. *B. japonica aurea* is golden leaved.

Prune: trim in spring.

Propagate: cuttings in autumn.

Caragana (Siberian Pea Tree, Chinese Pea Tree) (D). These are excellent shrubs for towns, and they do not mind about soil or position. *C. frutescens* grows about 3 ft. high, and has bright yellow pea-shaped flowers in April. *C. gerardiana* blooms in May, either cream colour or pale yellow, about 2 to 3 ft.

Prune: not necessary.

Propagate: layering in autumn.

Diervilla (Weigela, Bush Honeysuckle) (D). All the *Diervillas* are hardy and free growing. They like sun and ordinary soil. *D. grandiflora* bears a wealth of pink bloom in early June, and remains in flower for a long time. It is about 6 ft. high, and one of the most attractive. There are many other varieties, ranging in colour from white to claret-red. *D. middendorfiana*, a yellow in midsummer, grows 4 ft., and another of the later flowering varieties is Eva Rathke, with an abundance of deep crimson flowers that remain until quite late in the autumn.

Prune: remove old wood, and shorten shoots which have borne flowers.

Propagate: cuttings in autumn.

Hydrangea paniculata (D). This is perhaps the best for towns, although others will also grow under the same conditions. This one is attractive with its great white pointed heads of flowers in summer, reaching about 5 ft. high. Incidentally, the blooms, like other hydrangeas, turn most beautiful colours in autumn as they are dying. These turn umber, cream and bronze. They are most useful for indoor decoration, and a bowl of them picked at this stage will last for many weeks, and although having an almost artificial look, it is an attractive ''artificiality'', and not that dry, brittle, papery look of statice and immortelles. They should, of course, be placed in water, although they won't drink a great deal.

Prune: lightly trim previous year's shoots.

Propagate: cuttings in autumn.

Hippophæ rhamnoides (Sea Buckthorn, Sallow Thorn) (D). Although this is usually grown by the sea, it will thrive equally well in towns. It is quite hardy, and grows in ordinary soil. The male plants must be grown among the females, otherwise there will be no berries, and it is for the bright orange berries that the shrub is most valuable. It grows about 8 ft. high.

Prune: not necessary.

Propagate: layering in autumn.

Lespedeza (Bush Clover, Japanese Clover) (D). This hardy shrub is not often seen in towns, but it will grow under city conditions quite satisfactorily. *L. bicolour* is purplish-red in September, about 3 ft. *L. juncea* is blue and white in the same month, and the same height.

Prune: lightly after flowering.

Propagate: cuttings in spring.

Paulownia imperialis (D). This hardy tree must be included, for it is good in cities, although somewhat big, but the size (it may grow up to 30 ft). can be controlled by pruning. It has very pretty downy-looking leaves, and violet flowers in June. It will grow in ordinary soil, and sun or shade.

Prune: do not prune if flowers are required.

Propagate: cuttings in spring.

Prunus amygdalus (Almond). The well-known almond trees are a joy in cities in the spring with their beautiful rosy blossom, and later their bright, fresh little leaves. They are quite hardy, and enjoy ordinary soil. They bloom from March onwards, and grow up to 20 ft.

Prune: cut out old and dead wood after flowering.

Propagate: they are best bought in pots.

Pyrus aucuparia (Mountain Ash, Rowan Tree) (D). The lovely little Rowans are well known, and are supposed to be magic trees and to bring good fortune to the owner and the house. They are certainly always a reminder of faraway hill-sides and the tangle of bronze bracken, the wreaths of bramble burnished and berry-laden, and the haunt of rabbit and pheasant. They flourish their creamy flower heads in May, and their bright scarlet fruit in autumn. They will grow up to 30 ft., and are happy in ordinary soil, with preferably sun. There are also other attractive members of the *Pyrus* family suitable for towns.

Prune: not necessary.

Propagate: cuttings in autumn.

Ruscus aculeatus (Butcher's Broom, Knee Holly) (E), This hardy shrub is somewhat humble in appearance, maybe even a little dull, but it is useful for places where other things refuse to grow. It has nice dark green leaves, green flowers in May, and in winter red berries. It will grow anywhere, sun or shade, and under dripping trees.

Prune: lightly in spring.

Propagate: suckers in autumn.

Rosa. There should be more roses grown in cities. There are quite a considerable number which will thrive, and their beauty is not seen enough in our grey towns, perhaps because the majority of people are a little afraid of them. But, indeed, they are no more difficult than other shrubs.

The *Wichuriana* rambler, Dr. van Fleet, is a very good choice, and a lovely rose, being a soft rosy pink, and very vigorous. The hybrid tea roses, Betty Uprichard, Caroline Testout and Etoile de Hollande, all well known, and all attractive, will do in cities. The first is a lovely copper-salmon, while Caroline Testout is bright pink, and the last is a deep bright red—a beauty. There are, of course, plenty of others, and a good rose-grower should be consulted when buying.

Sarococca humilis (E). This little shrub has fragrant white flowers in early spring, and is charming in a town garden. It reaches about 2 ft., will grow in ordinary soil, sun or shade, and under the drip of trees.

Prune: not necessary.

Propagate: cuttings in autumn.

Symphoricarpus racemosus (Snow Berry). This is another shrub which does not mind where it is put, and obligingly bears pink flowers in July, and later white berries. It grows about 8 ft. high, and the bees are very fond of the blossoms.

Prune: thin out old wood in autumn.

Propagate: cuttings in autumn.

The following will also be found suitable for cities, and they have already been fully explained in earlier chapters:

Azara Microphylla.	Laburnum.
Berberis.	Lavandula.
Buddleia.	Phillyrea.
Choisya.	Pyracantha.
Clematis.	Philadelphus.
Cotoneaster.	Rhododendron.
Cratageus.	Ribes.
Cydonia.	Rosmarinus.
Cytisus.	Spiræa.
Daphne.	Syringa.
Euonymus.	Skimmia.
Escallonia.	Viburnum.
Hypericum.	Vinca.
Jasminum.	Vitis.
Kerria.	Wistaria.

CHAPTER EIGHT

HEDGES

IN spite of the very wide choice of shrubs, hedges are still inclined to be dull. This is a pity, for a hedge can be such a beautiful thing, and although in present times the more ornamental are a little more expensive, they are well worth the extra money. After all, a hedge can be a joy for ever or an eyesore which worries one year after year. It cannot be lightly ripped up and replaced, as in the case of a single shrub. Therefore when planting a hedge, let us always remember that we may have to live with it for a long time, and let us make it as beautiful as possible.

It must be borne in mind when planting that the hedge may be for pure ornament, or it may be just a useful fellow. Which is it to be ? Is it to shelter our vegetables and more precious plants from cold winds, or is it just for its own beauty ? For the former there is not quite so much choice, although that will depend largely on the situation. For the latter there is a wide choice.

It is important to choose something which is reasonably quick growing. A yew hedge is one of the most perfect, after years, but it takes many years to reach that stage of perfection. An evergreen is nearly always preferable to deciduous, and something, of course, should be chosen which will grow to the height required.

A very attractive hedge is a mixed one, made up of several flowering shrubs which will bloom at different times of the year, and interspersed with evergreens. But this usually takes a good amount of space, and is too large for the small garden.

93

Hedges should be carefully planted, and the ground well trenched and manured to commence with. If a very thick hedge is required, two rows of shrubs may be put in. Perhaps the most important thing for hedges is to keep them well pruned, particularly in their youth, so that they do not rush up, leaving behind long, gawky, ugly legs. A great part of the beauty of a hedge is the thickness from the ground upwards, with no gaps and straggly branches.

HEDGES

Berberis Darwinii (E). A berberis hedge is one of the most beautiful, for it provides interest and colour all the year round. If there is room, the hedge is far lovelier if allowed to grow free and unpruned, but otherwise it can be trimmed back moderately. *Darwinii* has orange and red flowers in May, and later on, plum-coloured berries. The spikes, like many of the barberries, are horribly long and sharp, and gloves should always be worn when tackling it. *B. stenophylla* is another good one for a hedge, also evergreen, with golden flowers in May, followed by black berries. Both grow up to about 7 or 8 ft. See also other chapters in which *Berberis* is mentioned.

Buxus sempervirens (Tree Box) (E). This never makes a very big hedge, and is rather slow growing. There are several nice varieties, of which *argentea* (the silver leaved) is attractive, and *myrtifolia* (myrtle-leaved) is also worth planting. The box hedges and edgings always remind me of the grand old kitchen gardens of old houses, with their neat edgings and that faint, indescribable scent of the foliage. They seem somehow to belong very much to the past, and to the grace of the late 17th century, with its formal gardens and topiary work. Box is useful on chalk soil, for there it thrives well. It should be kept clipped to a neat shape. See also ''City Gardens.''

Carpinus betulus (Hornbeam) (D). This makes a most excellent hedge, especially for exposed positions. It is rather similar to beech, but it is preferable, for it is not such a greedy feeder, and will not rob other plants near it, as beech does. The leaves remain on for a very long time, and in spring they are a charming olive green, turning in autumn to bronze and yellow. When in flower, it appears to be hung all over with little gold and silver tassels—the male and female catkins, or flowers, which, to be correct, they are. Birds are very fond of the nuts. It will grow in any ordinary soil, but doesn't take very kindly to chalk.

Prune: closely in autumn.

Propagate: seeds in autumn.

Cassinia leptophylla (E). For a small neat hedge, this shrub looks most attractive, and should be left unpruned. It will reach about 5 to 6 ft. See also "Dwarfs."

Cotoneaster Simonsi (D). Apart from being deciduous, it is one of the best for an informal hedge, and can be mixed with an evergreen to advantage. It is covered with white flowers in April, and later in the year gloriously scarlet berries. It will go up to 10 ft. See also "Climbers" and "Dwarfs."

Cratægus oxyacantha (The Common Hawthorn, White-thorn or Quick) (D). It is said to have first been used for hedges in the 17th century, when the Flemish farmers started hedging the farms in Norfolk. Actually it was used earlier than this, but not to any great extent, for it was not until the middle of the 18th century that many fields were enclosed by hedges. Until then they were just bounded by rough banks or ditches. May blossom is too well known to need any description, as also are its sharp thorns, and scarlet haws in autumn. In the language of flowers, it means Hope, which is indeed a pertinent name for it, blooming as it does after the long winter, and bringing all the hope for the coming season. The Glastonbury Thorn is a very early flowering one (*C. monogyna præcox*). See also "Fragrant."

Prune: budding or grafting.

Propagate: trim in late autumn.

Cupressus Lawsoniana (Lawson's Cypress) (E). This is one of the more ordinary hedge plants, as is *C. macrocarpa* (The Monterey Cypress), also evergreen. Nevertheless, they are sometimes very useful, especially on chalk soils, or by the sea, or where it is too exposed for more tender things. They are also quite quick growing, and always look neat. *Macrocarpa* makes a good substitute for a yew hedge, forming a nice dark, thick background for flowers. It should never be allowed to grow high and straggly, or it will snap off in a gale.

Prune: trim in spring and autumn.

Propagate: cuttings in autumn.

Cydonia Maulei (D). These look very charming grown as standards at intervals in a small low hedge. They have scarlet flowers in May, and grow 3 to 4 ft. high. Other varieties can be planted in the same manner in taller hedges and, being strong and shrubby, they give support to less vigorous things. See also "Climbers" and "Fragrant."

Cytisus. I once grew a row of brooms in a mixed hedge, and the effect was unusual and delightful. They must, of course, be mixed with other shrubs, and allowed to grow naturally, or just very lightly trimmed to keep shape. A hedge such as this needs a fair amount of space. See also "Fragrant" and "Dwarfs."

Escallonia. Excellent for mild districts or by the sea. In the case of hedges, they should be trimmed after flowering. *E. exoniensis* has rosy tinted flowers in June, and grows about 15 ft. *E. organensis* is red in September, about 6 ft. These are both evergreen, and there is a wide range from which to choose. See also "Fragrant."

Euonymus japonicus (E). This has shiny bright leaves

which turn bright colours in autumn. The fruits stay on the tree long after the leaves and cover it with orange and pink. The greeny white flowers appear in May. It grows about 6 ft. high. See also "Dwarfs."

Fuchsia Riccartonii (D). This makes one of the most beautiful hedges, and I cannot understand why it is not more often seen. In catalogues it is sometimes listed as half-hardy, but it will stand anything except an absolutely abnormal winter. It has bright scarlet flowers in summer, beautifully tinted leaves and red stems. It is useful, too, for cutting, lasting well in the house, and its drooping and graceful branches lending themselves well to decoration. It will grow up to about 10 ft. It is a reasonably quick grower, and will soon make a thick hedge. It needs a little space, for it should be allowed to grow as freely as possible, to show off the beauty of its form and flowers. Fuchsias have a charm and dusky mystery particularly their own, and they remind me always of the beautiful counties of Devon and Dorset, where they grow practically wild. I think these hardy ones are far more attractive than their pampered greenhouse brothers. They make a very good hedge between flower and kitchen garden. See also "Dwarfs."

Ilex (Holly) (E). Holly is a well-known favourite, and certainly makes a good hedge, but it takes quite a long time to make into a really large one. When it is mature, it makes a wonderful wind-break in exposed places and forms an excellent shelter but, as I say, it does take time. It must also be kept perfectly trimmed, or it loses most of its charm. It is rather attractive planted here and there with *Berberis*. There are a great number from which to make a choice. *I. aurea regina* (Golden Queen) is one of the golden leaved varieties, and *I. argentea medio-picta* (The Silver Milkmaid) one of the silvers. They are all quite hardy.

Prune: trim spring and autumn.

Propagate: cuttings with a heel.

Lavendula (E). There are many charming lavenders which make a pretty little hedge, or rather division, of one part of the garden from another. It is important that they be kept neatly trimmed, otherwise they tend to grow untidy and scraggy, and have to be replaced by younger plants. They make a good division to a kitchen garden, and can be given extra height if grown on a small raised bed. See also "Fragrant."

Lonicera. Some of the deciduous shrubby honeysuckles look very charming in a mixed hedge. *L. Nitida*, an evergreen, is one most usually grown as a hedge. It is moderately quick in growth, and makes a compact, thick hedge. This is best grown alone. There is quite a range from which to choose, and it is as well to consult a nurseryman before buying. *L. Nitida* should be clipped in June. See also "Fragrant."

Olearia Haastii (E). The Daisy Bush makes a charming hedge, and grows at about the rate of a foot a year. Being rather on the half-hardy side, it is not suitable for a very exposed position, or for the North of England.

Prune: it should be trimmed in spring.

See also "Fragrant."

Osmanthus aquifolium (syn. *Olea ilicifolia*) (E). This is a hardy creature, very useful to form a thick screen, and fairly quick growing. It is a little like a holly in appearance, and will grow up to 10 ft. It needs no pruning except to have any straggly shoots cut back in June. See also "Fragrant."

Phillyrea (E). See "Fragrant."

Pyracantha. A mixed hedge will look delightful with the addition of some *Pyracanthas* here and there, but it will have to be in a reasonably warm position. See also "Climbers."

Prunus spinosa (Sloe, Blackthorn) (D). This makes a good thick hedge, even though it is deciduous. Its twisty, interlacing branches form a dense barrier, and a sharp one to the unwary, with its thorns on the end of each twig. The flowers come before the leaves, a far purer white than the Whitethorn, and giving the bushes the appearance of a white cloud of snow. It is very beautiful in March in all its glory against the dark, unawakened branches of other shrubs. The little sloes in autumn look as if formed from dark blue wax, and are rather bitter. It will make a hedge 10 ft. high, and requires trimming in autumn. It is excellent for an exposed, cold position.

Propagation: cuttings in autumn.

Ribes (D). The ordinary pink flowering currant, *R. sanguineum*, makes an attractive hedge, but needs a good deal of space, as it does not want to be cut back too drastically to be seen at its best. It grows quickly, and makes a pretty boundary to an orchard. See also "Fragrant."

Prune: just lightly shorten the shoots after flowering.

Ruscus aculeatus (Butcher's Broom, Knee Holly) (E). A suitable hedge shrub, very hardy, and no trouble to look after. See also "City Gardens."

Rosa. There is no more exquisite hedge than one composed of the Sweet Briars, *R. rubiginosa*. I have already mentioned them in the chapter on "Fragrant" shrubs, but I add them yet again as a reminder that, if it is possible, they should be grown in every garden, and grown as a hedge; they take up little space and, even where space is limited, something less precious should be sacrificed for them. They are particularly charming when grown to divide off a rose garden, or one part of the flower garden from another. There are other beautiful roses, too, which make, to my mind, the most lovely of all hedges. The *Rugosa* roses are charming, and also the Hybrid Musks, such as Pax, a very vigorous white, with a lovely fragrance ; Felicia, which is somewhat smaller, a lovely yellowy-pink, produced in many clusters of little rosettes, and Penelope, which is one of, if not the best of all. It has a delicate salmon tint, a lovely scent, and flowers a long time. Zéphirine Drouhin, a hybrid Bourbon, is another good hedge one, with bright pink blooms, and very fragrant. This should not be pruned much, but just thinned a little, and dead wood removed. In fact, all these roses are best left alone as much as possible, and allowed to grow naturally.

Rosmarinus. For a small hedge, this can be very delightful. See "Fragrant."

Rhododendron. When Rhododendrons are grown as hedges, there must be ample space for them, so that they are well shown off, and not cut back more than absolutely necessary. For this, a good deal of space is required, and I would not recommend them for the small garden, where they look cramped and out of place. A nurseryman should be consulted when choosing.

Rhus cotinoides (Sumach, Smoke Tree, Wig Tree, American Smoke Tree) (D). This hardy and most interesting shrub may be grown together to form a hedge, although they must be allowed to grow more or less at will. *R. cotinoides* (the American one) grows about 8 ft. high, and the flower stalks are all covered with little hairs, giving the bush a smoky appearance. The leaves turn the most brilliant and glorious colours in autumn. *R. cotinus* (The Smoke Tree, Wig Tree, or Venetian Sumach) grows taller, sometimes up to 12 ft., but has the same hairy stalks and smoky look. They are happy in ordinary soil, preferably a sunny position, and are hardy.

Prune: very lightly, just to keep shape.

Propagate: cuttings in autumn.

Rhamnus (Buckthorn) (E and D). These are all hardy, and are good for windy places or for the seaside. They do in ordinary soil, in sun or shade. *R. alaternus* grows about 15 ft., and is a good kind, as it is evergreen. Of the deciduous, *R. cathartica* (Buckthorn), grows about 8 ft.

Prune: only keep tidy.

Propagate: layering in autumn.

Santolina (Lavender Cotton) (E). These hardy little plants make a nice little hedge like lavender or rosemary. They will grow in any ordinary soil, and preferably in sun. *S. Chamæcyparissus* (*S. incana*) has bright little yellow flowers in July, and grows about 2 to 3 ft. high. Its leaves are rather attractive with their covering of greyish down, of a somewhat cottony texture.

Prune: just keep neat.

Propagate: cuttings in spring.

Staphylea (Bladder Nut, St. Antony's Nut) (D). These shrubs are hardy, and form a very good wind-break, but are not suitable for a small garden. *S. colchica* has white flowers in summer, and grows about 8 ft. high. *S. pinnata* (St. Antony's Nut) is also white, in May, and from 10 to 15 ft. high. They like sun, but otherwise do well in any ordinary soil.

Prune: just trim straggly shoots when flowers are over.

Propagate: cuttings in autumn.

Thuya. There are several of these suitable for hedges. *T. plicata* and *T. orientalis* are both good, and make hedges of about 5 ft. The foliage is very similar to that of the Cupressus. They are no trouble, will grow anywhere, and make a good thick evergreen screen. These again make a good substitute for a yew hedge, being much quicker in growth. They will do in any position or soil. See also "Dwarfs."

Prune: trim in autumn.

Propagate: cuttings in autumn.

Taxus (Yew). Yew hedges are too well known to need any description, and indeed are extremely beautiful with their dark colouring, which makes such a beautiful background for other plants. As I have mentioned before, the only thing against them is that thay do take rather a long time to grow big. One can of course buy fairly large bushes, but if too big, they are somewhat liable to resent the disturbance, and die on one's hands. The one commonly used for hedges is *T. baccata* (The Common Yew), but there are other kinds which also make charming hedges. *Aurea* (The Golden Yew) is lovely in its way, although not so effective, I think, as the ordinary one. Also, *fastigiata* (The Irish Yew) makes a good hedge. They will grow happily in ordinary soil, but like it well drained. They like moisture, but don't like their feet in a perpetual sort of bog. I once planted some yews, some of which appeared very sickly and eventually died. It was discovered later, they were on top of a natural spring!

Prune: they should be trimmed into shape in spring or autumn.

Propagate: cuttings in autumn.

Ulex. Gorse makes a thick and impenetrable hedge. It can be very much nicer than it sounds, when properly trimmed and cared for. The best for a hedge is *U. europæus flore-pleno*, growing 6 ft. high, and splendid in spring when covered with its bright gold double flowers. It has an added advantage in being an evergreen, and is excellent to form the boundary of a kitchen garden, or orchard, or field. It must not, however, be allowed to ramble at will, or it will become untidy and straggly. See also "Dwarfs" and "Fragrant."

Vaccinum (Whortleberry, Bilberry, Huckleberry) (E and D). These hardy, well-known shrubs look delightful in a mixed hedge, but they really require some other things of a somewhat stronger and sturdier growth intermingled. *V. myrtillus* (The Bilberry or Whortleberry) has pale pink flowers in May and grows up to about only 2 ft., but I have seen it planted as a little dividing hedge on top of a bank in a kitchen garden, and very pretty it was. It is deciduous, and the leaves turn lovely tints in the autumn. *V. orymc-bosum* has pink flowers in May and grows about 8 to 10 ft. *V. padifolium* has attractive yellow and wine coloured flowers in June, growing about 8 ft. high. Of the evergreens, *V. ovatum* has white flowers and grows the same height. They all have berries in autumn. The colours vary from red to blue or almost black. They will grow in any soil or position, but prefer peat.

Prune: just keep trimmed a nice shape with the hedge.
Propagate: cuttings in summer.

SOME OTHER CHARACTERS

104

CHAPTER NINE

SOME OTHER CHARACTERS

IN this last chapter I have gathered together some other characters which will not lend themselves to cataloguing under any particular heading. Each has its own especial individuality, its own very definite character, be it simple and sweet, strong and mysterious, or just rather difficult to describe, unless you know it as you know a friend.

Take, for instance, *Camellia*. There's a lady fine and fair ; a great beauty, with perhaps, the most romantic character of all. Hers are the memories of bygone leisure and grace ; memories of heavy rustling silks that swept against her leaves, of little white hands which plucked her blooms . . . How can you place her in a border with a mixed company, or against a wall of a villa ? Sacrilege. She must have a place just right for her: a sweeping velvet-smooth lawn, neighbours at a distance, and dignity about her. If the setting be not perfect, rather then leave her to some other luckier gardener, and buy a more simple person who will look at home.

Take now a more simple creature. *Cornus*, the Dogberry or Dogwood. Yet that again has entirely its own character which needs just the right position for it to be "something," and not just a bush. The great beauty of the Dogwood is the simple, exquisite line, and bold colour. It is like a quick sketch by a great artist. Nothing superfluous, nothing meaningless. Put it among other things, in a maze of bushes and evergreens, and it becomes just one of them. Put it alone, or rather, a whole colony of them on their own, at the edge of a meadow, or on the fringe of

E

a wild garden, and there in autumn its blood-red leaves, and in winter its vivid scarlet stems, are something . . . something to wonder upon.

Out of this gathering of characters, the gardener must discover his particular loves ; he must discover for himself the particular background which is the perfect setting for each jewel. Neither I nor anyone else can really advise where they should be grown unless we know the garden in which they are to be placed.

The Great Artist who designed all these beautiful things made also the right place for them.

SOME OTHER CHARACTERS

Arbutus Andrachne (Strawberry Tree) (E). This attractive shrub will be found suitable for many gardens and positions, for it is happy in ordinary soil, a little shelter, and sun. It is at home in either a small or large garden. They do best of all in a moist, peaty soil. *A. Andrachne* is one of the most showy, with greeny white flowers in April and bright fruit in autumn, while the young shoots are tinged red. *A. Unedo* is perhaps the better known. It grows about the same height as the former, 10 to 15 ft., and has rather whiter, bell-shaped flowers. The fruits of all the Arbutuses are very like strawberries.

Prune: not necessary.

Propagate: budding in summer.

Abutilon vitifolium (Indian Mallow) (E). This shrub is half-hardy, but it is worth protecting in winter, and planting in a warm sheltered position, for it is unusual and showy, while the flowers continue for a long time. It is a very lovely blue in July, and is the most hardy of them all. The blooms are bell-shaped and drooping in a very graceful manner. It grows about 4 ft. high, and does best in a

106

peaty soil. It is quite safe in a mild district in the south of England.

Prune: not necessary.

Propagate: cuttings in greenhouse in spring.

Betula nana (Dwarf Silver Birch) (D). This tiny beauty, member of a family of trees only to be compared with the Willows for grace and beauty, grows only 3 ft. high. It is perfect for small or large garden, and should be placed in a position of honour where it may be admired from all angles. It is no trouble, will grow in ordinary soil.

Prune: not necessary.

Propagate: seeds in spring.

Cæsalpinia japonica (syn. *C. sepiaria*) (D). It is strange that this hardy and very attractive shrub is not more often seen in gardens. It looks best when three or four plants are massed together. It has very shiny green leaves, and bears an abundance of rich yellow flowers in spring. Grows about 6 ft. high. It does not demand any particular position to show off its beauty, and will do in any soil, although it prefers peat and sun, and dislikes cold winds.

Prune: just trim to keep a nice shape.

Propagate: seeds in a frame any time.

Callicarpa japonica (French Mulberry, Purple Mulberry) (D). This is a very pretty little shrub, and although it should be placed by a sheltered wall, it is hardy in mild districts. It has pale pink blossoms in August, and in late autumn lovely dark violet berries. It grows about 4 ft. in ordinary soil.

Prune: previous year's growth in spring.

Propagate: cuttings in August.

Camellia (Tea Plant) (E). The foliage of *Camellias* matches the blooms in exquisite form and colour. It makes a perfect setting, shiny and dark, for the beautiful waxy blooms. It can be said without exaggeration that the Camellia is almost the loveliest of all shrubs. It is

107

often called half-hardy, but is really much stronger than is generally imagined. The only things Camellias dislike are strong cold winds, and strong sun sometimes spoils their blooms. There is no reason why they should not do well anywhere in south England. In a bad winter they can be protected when young if necessary, but once they are established, they will be no trouble. They definitely dislike lime, and thrive wonderfully in peat and leaf mould. It is as well for them to have a little shade to protect the blooms. The following, out of many lovelies, I would strongly recommend:—*C. cuspidata*, with white waxen blooms in May, growing about 6 ft. *C. japonica*, brilliant red flowers in May, but growing up to 15 ft. This is the ordinary one, and the mother of many beautiful single and double varieties. *C. Sasanqua* unfolds pure white blooms as early as February, and consequently has to be watched for frosts. It grows 6 ft. high.

Prune: just tidy straggly shoots after flowering.

Propagate: cuttings in greenhouse in August.

Caryopteris mastacanthus (Moustache Plant). This is a half-hardy shrubby perennial, and exceedingly attractive, for it has lavender-blue flowers rather like spiræa, in autumn. It must be included for this alone, for flowering shrubby things are rather scarce at that time of the year, and it gives welcome colour at a time when colour is precious. It should be grown by a warm sheltered wall, or at the back of a sunny border safe from cold winds. It grows about 5 ft. high. It is happy in ordinary soil, although peat is all the better for it.

Prune: not necessary.

Propagate: cuttings in spring.

Catalpa bigonioides (Indian Bean Tree) (D). This is a sturdy, handsome creature, prepared to flourish in poor soil, where other things would refuse to grow. It is too big for a small garden, growing eventually up to 20 ft., or more sometimes. Of course, it can be kept within bounds by pruning, nevertheless it is a hearty feeder and would rob the soil too much in a small place. It has whitish flowers, blotched with purple and yellow, and the leaves are a very bright green, with a bronzy tint at the edges. It is sometimes seen in London square gardens, where it defiantly flourishes great heads of blossom to the dusty air.

Prune: not necessary unless to keep fairly small.

Propagate: cuttings in summer.

Ceratostigma Willmottianum (Lead-wort). It has most brilliant azure blue flowers in July, the loveliest blue imaginable. It has the disadvantage of dying right back in winter, but it springs up again in the New Year. It grows up to about 6 ft. It prefers a sandy loam, and is quite hardy. Really, this is one of the gems of the shrub world.

Prune: not necessary.

Propagate: cuttings in August.

Cercis (Judas Tree, Red-bud) (D). This hardy chap needs a fair amount of space. *C. canadensis* (Red-bud) grows up to 30 ft., although the more usual size for it is about 12 ft. It has rosy flowers in May. *C. siliquastrum* (The Judas Tree) will reach 20 ft. in time, but like the former it is very slow growing, and will remain a charming little bush (or tree) for a long while. This one is a purplish-rose in May. The flowers are very pretty, like peas, and simply cover the bushes as though they were covered by a million tiny butterflies. They enjoy a rich deep soil, preferably sandy, and a sheltered shrubbery.

Prune: old branches in spring.

Propagate: layering in autumn.

Clianthus puniceus (Glory Pea, Lobster Claw, Parrot's Bill) (D). This odd and attractive shrub is delicate and will only do in a very sheltered spot in a warm part of southern England. It grows about 6 ft. high and has bright crimson flowers in May. It needs loam and leaf mould to be happy, and it is useless to plant it unless your garden be really warm and sheltered.

Prune: shorten young shoots in spring.

Propagate: cuttings in greenhouse in spring.

Colutea arborescens (Bladder Senna) (D). This is a useful hardy shrub which will grow almost anywhere, in a damp or dry position, and seems to flower almost better in a poor soil. It has yellow flowers in August and grows 10 ft. high. It is rather similar to a Broom, and the seed pods in autumn are bladder-like, changing in colour from red to orange and yellow.

Prune: if cut hard back every other spring, they flower better.

Propagate: cuttings in autumn.

Cornus (Dogwood, Bunch Berry, Dogberry, Cornelian Cherry) (D). I have already spoken of the beauty of the Dogwoods. There are many from which to choose, and the following are two of the best, to my mind:—*C. sibirica*, with its glowing red stems, and *C. sanguinea* (the ordinary Dogwood), also with brilliant scarlet stems. Both grow to about 8 ft. in height, and should be cut to the ground in early spring, about February, for it is the new young wood which has the most beautiful colour. They will grow in ordinary soil and in any position.

Prune: branches can be cut into shape in autumn as well as the hard cutting back in spring.

Propagate: cuttings in autumn.

Corokia buddleoides (E). This is a shrub not often seen, but it certainly has character, with its queer corky-looking, rather twisty branches, and bright yellow flowers in summer. It grows about 8 ft. high, in ordinary soil, and does best with the protection of a south or west wall. It is half-hardy, and needs protection in winter.

Prune: not necessary.

Propagate: cuttings in autumn.

110

Coronilla Emerus (Crown Vetch, Scorpion Senna) (D). This has red and yellow flowers in April, and grows about 8 ft. high. It is hardy, but should be given a fairly sheltered position in a shrubbery. It will do in ordinary soil, and likes a sunny place.

Prune: straggly shoots after flowering.

Propagate: cuttings in autumn.

Desfontainea spinosa (E). This is sometimes regarded as half hardy, but it is perfectly hardy in a mild district. It might tend to be a little tender in the north of England. It is rather similar in some ways to a Holly, for it is sturdy, and has dark, shiny, spiny leaves. The flowers in August are drooping, scarlet and yellow, and are produced in great abundance. It grows about 4 ft. high, and likes a peaty soil. It is as well to plant it in a sheltered position.

Prune: not necessary.

Propagate: cuttings in spring.

Enkianthus campanulatus (D). This shrub is definitely a lime hater, and it is hopeless to try to grow it in a limy soil. It is very pretty with red flowers in summer, and in the autumn the foliage turns most beautiful colours. It grows about 6 ft. high, in ordinary soil, preferably a slightly moist position.

Prune: not necessary.

Propagate: cuttings in spring.

Eucryphia pinnatifolia (E). Sometimes this shrub is deciduous, or partly so, but it is very attractive and unusual. It has snow-white flowers, with gilty stamens in the centre in August, and the leaves are attractive, turning crimson and bronze, in autumn. It is an exquisite thing when it is covered in summer with its cloud of blossom. It is rather like a bush of wild roses. It does best in a rich, well-drained soil, and a sheltered position with plenty of sun.

Prune: not necessary.

Propagate: layering in autumn.

Eupatorium cannabium (Hemp Agrimony). This is more of a shrubby perennial, the true shrubs being greenhouse ones, but it is worth growing, for it is hardy and will do in ordinary soil. It has purplish red flowers in July, and grows about 3 ft. It looks well in the front of a mixed shrubbery.

Prune: not necessary.

Propagate: division in spring.

Euphorbia (Spurge, Poinsettia, etc.). Of the hardy species, *E. Cyparissias* (The Cypress Spurge) is attractive, with yellow flowers in June, growing about 2 to 3 ft. high. It is hardy, grows in ordinary soil, likes a dry, sunny position.

Prune: not necessary.

Propagate: cuttings in autumn.

Exochorda racemosa (syns. *E. grandiflora and Spiræa grandiflora*) (The Pearl Bush) (D). This is a very beautiful shrub indeed. In May it is covered with beads of white, rather like ropes of pearls. It should be in every garden, for it is easy to grow, demanding only ordinary well-drained soil, and content to show off its beauty in shrubbery or odd corner. It grows 6 ft.

Prune: lightly after flowering.

Propagate: cuttings in summer.

Fabiana imbricata (False Heath) (E). This, as its name suggests, is rather similar to heather, but is really a member of the solanum family. It is quite hardy, and bears a large number of tiny white flowers in May, growing about 3 ft. It might be a trifle tender in the North. It will grow in ordinary soil, but will do better in peat.

Prune: not necessary.

Propagate: cuttings in spring.

Fendlera rupicola (D). This hardy shrub does well in a sandy loam. It has rosy-white flowers in May, and will grow up to about 5 ft. It is best in a rockery, or against a warm wall.

Prune: not necessary.

Propagate: cuttings in summer.

Fraxinus (Flowering Ash, Manna Ash) (D). The ordinary Ash tree will be found too large for most gardens, but there are one or two varieties which are smaller, and are charming in a moderately large garden. It has been well named the "Venus of the Woods", for it is indeed lovely with its slender, ashy-grey stems and elegant boughs. *F. excelsior pendula* (The Weeping Ash) is one of the loveliest of weeping trees and looks beautiful by the side of an ornamental lake. *F. e. aurea* is the Golden Ash, and might be grown for the sole sake of its bright golden bark in winter. In the ordinary way the Ash will grow from about 25 to 100 ft. high, which gives some idea of the room required for it. I have included it here, for some readers may have a large enough garden in which to enjoy its beauty, and I often hear people asking what trees they shall plant in a garden. It will grow in any soil or position, and is no trouble. It has white, green and yellow flowers, but they do not appear until the tree is fairly old—about thirty years, I think!

Prune: it can be kept within bounds by pruning occasionally.

Propagation: grafting in spring.

Ginkgo (Ginko Tree, Maidenhair Tree) (D). *G. biloba* (syn. *Salisburia adiantifolia*). This is a most distinctive and interesting character, which is rarely seen in gardens, but which might be grown with profit, for it is hardy, will grow in any soil or position, and is quite unlike any other tree I have ever seen. There is no need to be frightened by the term "tree," either, for it is a slow grower. I understand it will grow to 60 ft., but I had one which only grew about 6 ft. in ten or eleven years, and even then took up little room, for it is of neat habit, and while one could hardly call it slender, as for instance, a birch or willow, it is slim and upright, in a thicker way. The leaves are like big Maidenhair Fern leaves, being fan shaped, and light in colour, turning a clear yellow in autumn. Little greeny yellow male and female flowers are borne on separate trees.

Prune: not necessary.

Propagate: seeds in autumn.

Halesia carolina (syn. *tetraptera*) (Silver Bell, Snowdrop Tree) (D). This is a very beautiful shrub, rather similar to *Styrax Obassia*. It has little snowdrop-like flowers in May, glistening-white, and will grow up to 15 ft. It likes the sunshine, and although quite hardy, is better in a sheltered border or shrubbery.

Prune: keep a neat shape after flowering.

Propagate: cuttings in autumn.

Halimodendron argenteum (Salt Tree) (D). This shrub has the most attractive leaves, all downy white, and shaped like feathers. It has purple flowers in June, and grows about 5 ft. high. It prefers a sandy soil, and sun or shade, in shrubbery or border.

Prune: just shape up in autumn.

Propagate: cuttings in late autumn.

Gleditschia triacanthos (Honey Locust, Water Locust) (D). This is another character, both interesting and lovely, which is rarely seen, and why I know not, for it is hardy and easy to grow, and would be a change from some of the lilacs and laburnums in the ordinary garden. Try to acquire one of these by hook or by crook—I know you will not be disappointed. It has sharp spikes, of which one has to beware when tending it. The little green flowers appear in summer, and the foliage is in fronds of feathers, bright green when young, turning yellow in the autumn. The little browny-green pods are interesting. There is also *G. aquatica* (syns. *G. monosperma* and *inermis*) (The Water

Locust). This is a little smaller than the former, but both may eventually grow up to 30 ft., although they are rather slow growing. They like ordinary soil, and a sheltered border or shrubbery.

Prune: not necessary.

Propagate: seeds in spring.

Grevillea sulphurea (The Silk Bark Oak) (E). This is the only one really hardy enough to be recommended for outside, and even that requires a mild district to do well. *G. rosmarinifolia* is also grown outside in very warm places but it is rather more tender. I would reccommend it if you don't mind cosseting it a bit, and covering it up in the winter. *Sulphurea* has yellow flowers in summer and grows about 10 ft. *Rosmarinifolia* has scarlet blooms also in summer, and is 6 ft. high. The flowers are rather queer and clawlike. The leaves of the latter, as indicated, are like rosemary. They both enjoy peaty soil and shelter.

Prune: not necessary.

Propagate: layering in autumn.

Indigofera decora (Indigo) (D). The Indigos are unusual and attractive, although a little on the tender side in cold districts, where they should be placed in a warm position against a wall, and protected in winter. They like leaf mould and peat, and a well-drained border. *Decora* has white, crimson and pink flowers in July, and grows about 2 ft. high. *I. Gerardiana* bears long racemes of red flowers, also summer, and about 6 ft. The flowers are very pretty little pea-shaped things, and cover the entire bushes, giving a very fine appearance of colour.

Prune: very lightly after flowering.

Propagate: cuttings in greenhouse in late summer.

Jamesia americana (D). This is a hardy, very pretty little shrub which is rarely seen. It is very useful, for it will stand the hardest winters without turning a hair, and brings forth each spring a multitude of clusters of snow-white flowers. It is useful if something slow growing is wanted, and it rarely reaches more than 4 ft. high. It has oval greyish leaves which set off the flowers well. It succeeds in ordinary soil.

Prune: lightly after flowering.

Propagate: cuttings in autumn.

Kalmia (Moutain Laurel, Calico Bush, American Laurel, Swamp Laurel, Sheep Laurel) (E and D). These are very pretty shrubs which enjoy the same situation as Rhododendrons, and abhor lime or chalk. They make neat bushes from 2 to 3 ft. high, and look well massed together, particularly with lilies growing between. They afford welcome shade for the lilies' feet, and there is the additional beauty of colour from both shrub and flowers, lasting a long time. *K. angustifolia* (The Sheep Laurel) has somewhat smaller flowers than the other Kalmias, but they are borne in abundance, and are a bright crimson in June. This is an evergreen. *K. glauca*, a deciduous, grows more freely, and also produces a great abundance of clusters of purply-lilac flowers in May. They are quite hardy, and no trouble to grow, apart from their dislike of lime.

Prune: not necessary.

Propagate: layering in spring.

Lantana (Jamaican Mountain Sage, Surinam Tea Plant) (E). This is worth growing, although very tender, and must be removed to the greenhouse for protection in the winter. It likes a rich sandy soil, and plenty of sunshine. The flowers are rather similar to those of Verbena, although a little smaller. They will bloom throughout the summer, and the colours of all of them are bold and brilliant. *L. Camara* is violet, and grows about 4 ft. *L. sellowiana* is a lilacy-pink, 3 ft.

Prune: not necessary.

Propagate: cuttings in the greenhouse in autumn.

Laurus nobilis (Bay Tree, Sweet Bay, Victor's Laurel,

Poet's Laurel) (E). It might be thought unnecessary to include the Bay Tree, for it is well known, and yet not as much planted as it might be. Perhaps its modest form is rather despised, and yet it is a beautiful and shapely shrub that is very much at home at the entrance to the kitchen garden. There, like some comely matron, it can spread its spruce neat skirt of green, and watch over the children of the kitchen plot. The dark lance-shaped leaves are beautiful in their quiet way, and are definitely of great use in the kitchen. It is also one of those useful creatures which will do well in tubs, if that be necessary. It will grow anywhere in any soil, and grows up to 20 ft. in time.

Prune: lightly to keep shape in spring, if necessary.

Propagate: cuttings in autumn.

Leycesteria formosa (Himalayan Honeysuckle, Flowering Nutmeg) (D). This old-fashioned shrub is not a showy one either, but it has a quiet charm all its own. Pheasants like the berries, and it is sometimes planted as a cover for game. It is not seen much in the modern garden. It is hardy, will grow in ordinary soil, and preferably sun. It has pendulous bunches of white flowers, tinged with purple, from June to August, and later, purple berries. It grows about 5 ft.

Prune: lightly in spring.

Propagate: cuttings in spring.

Mitraria coccinea (Mitre Flower, Scarlet Mitre Pod) (E). This is a very lovely climber, which used always to be grown in the cool greenhouse, but it has been found hardy enough to do out of doors if well protected in winter in a mild district and sunny position. It certainly does very much better in a greenhouse, but few of us can spare the space for such things nowadays, when there is probably only a small house at our disposal. It needs a peaty soil, a rather moist position, and above all, shelter. It blooms

117

in June, and sometimes continues to flower until the end of of August. The flowers are a vivid scarlet.

Prune: not necessary.

Propagate: cuttings in a frame in autumn.

Myricaria germanica (syn. *Tamarix Germanica*) (German Tamarisk) (D). This is a useful shrub for its hardiness and willingness to grow anywhere in any soil, preferring, if anything, an open sunny place. It bears pink flowers in July, and grows about 6 ft.

Prune: shape in spring.

Propagate: cuttings in autumn.

Nandina domestica (Heavenly Bamboo) (E). An unusual creature this, with a very misleading name, for it is not a Bamboo at all, but is related to the Berberis family. It is called by the Chinese the Sacred Bamboo, and is supposed to bring good fortune if planted near the house. The name probably arose because the long slim stems are somewhat cane, or bamboo like. Its greatest interest is perhaps the colour and form of the leaves, which are a beautiful red in autumn. It bears white flowers in summer, and grows 6 ft. high, but takes some time to reach that height, and is very much better when it has become established. It is more or less half-hardy and needs a sheltered place, but will grow in ordinary soil.

Prune: not necessary.

Propagate: cuttings in spring in the greenhouse.

Parrotia (Persian Iron Wood, Persian Witch Hazel) (D). This is another with particularly beautiful foliage in autumn. The leaves turn deep rich colours, and is invaluable for both garden and house decoration. *P. persica* has red flowers in March, and will grow up to 30 ft. *P. Jacquemontiana* is yellow in May and June, and is smaller, growing to about 12 or 15 ft. They are hardy and will grow in ordinary soil.

Prune: not necessary.

Propagate: layering in autumn.

Pittosporum crassifolium (Parchment Bark) (D). These are half-hardy, and need a well-drained border with sun and shelter. Some people advise lifting them in October and wintering them in the greenhouse. I have grown one in the south of England, in a warm locality, and it was left outside for years. It thrived. *Crassifolium* has purple flowers in spring, and grows up to 15 ft.

Prune: not necessary.

Propagate: cuttings in the greenhouse.

Plagianthus Lyalli (syn. *Gaya Lyalli*) (D). This is a most lovely shrub, full of character, and should be grown as a specimen on a lawn, or in some position where its full beauty may be seen to advantage. It has attractive heart-shaped leaves, and in summer snow-white flowers with gold stamens. It will eventually grow up to 20 ft. or so. Unfortunately it is half-hardy, and will not do in cold places, although sometimes it flourishes well in some Scottish gardens. It should, however, be placed in a sheltered position, and if possible in sandy soil with leaf mould.

Prune: lightly prune shoots which have flowered.

Propagate: cuttings in autumn.

Romneya Coulteri (Californian Poppy) (D). It is some-times classed as a hardy perennial, and it is liable to be cut down in winter by frosts, but it puts forth new shoots again in the spring, and is well worth growing. The beautiful white yellow-centred flowers appear in June, and sometimes continue until the end of September. It is fragrant, grows about 5 ft., and should be grown in peaty soil with the protection of a south wall.

Prune: not necessary.

Propagate: cuttings in spring in greenhouse.

Salix (Willow, Sallow, Osier, Withy) (D). These very

beautiful little trees should be found a place for, if possible. They are hardy and will grow in ordinary soil, although they prefer a damp place, particularly the Weeping Willow, which, to be at its best, should really be beside a stream or pond. Nevertheless, they will thrive happily in an ordinary garden, even in towns. It is a great help to them if they are given plenty of water in very dry weather. They look charming grown singly on a lawn, or in the middle of paving, where they should stand alone so that their perfection of form and delicacy may be admired. *S. caprea* (The Goat Willow), the common hedge willow, has catkins before the leaves appear, and grows up to 15 ft. The branches are a rather purply-brown, and it is the first willow to flower. *S. viminalis*, (the Osier Willow), is the one grown for osiers. When young, the branches have a soft, silky appearance, and as they grow older they appear polished. *S. babylonica* (The Weeping Willow) will grow up to 30 ft. high, and is to my mind the loveliest of a lovely family, with its delicate drooping branches—as lovely in mid-winter as in spring or summer. I make no apology for talking so long of what some people consider an ordinary tree, for it is one of the most beautiful things we may have in our gardens.

Prune: hardly ever necessary.

Propagate: cuttings in autumn.

Sophora japonica (Chinese Pagoda Tree) (D). This is a very graceful little tree. I say little, for although it will grow up to 50 ft., it remains small for a great number of years. It is hardy, although a sheltered lawn is the best place for it, and ordinary soil. It has creamy-sulphur coloured flowers in September. One I had never bloomed, and I believe they take a number of years before blooming.

Prune: lightly in spring if necessary.

Propagate: cuttings in late summer.

Stephanandra flexuosa (D). This hardy shrub delights

in a moist loam, and is well placed at the edge of a shrubbery or woodland garden. It is most beautiful for its very charming, fern-like foliage. It has greeny-white flowers in June, and grows about 6 ft. high. It is no trouble and has no particular likes.

Prune: not necessary.

Propagate: cuttings in late summer.

Stranvæsia glaucescens (E). A half-hardy shrub, which requires protection in winter and a sheltered spot. It likes sandy loam and warmth. The white flowers appear in July, and it grows about 15 ft. high.

Prune: not necessary.

Propagate: cuttings in the greenhouse.

Stuartia malachodendron (syn. *S. virginica*). Not a very well known shrub, perhaps because it will not do in every garden, being a little on the delicate side, nevertheless worth growing, if space is to spare. It hates east winds, and should be in a sheltered spot, preferably in a peaty soil. The flowers are white with purple anthers in July, and it grows 12 ft. high.

Prune: not necessary.

Propagate: layering in autumn.

Tricuspidaria lanceolata (E). This is sometimes called *Crinodendron*. It is half-hardy, and needs the shelter of a south wall. The rich crimson flowers come in June, sometimes a little later, and if the season is mild, they sometimes stay on a long time. I have known it come into bud very late in the year, and flower in the winter, but that perhaps was a freak, if a lovely one. It grows 12 ft. high, likes a peaty soil, and is hopeless in lime.

Prune: not necessary.

Propagate: cuttings in late summer.

Viburnum lantana (Wayfaring Tree) (D). I have already mentioned *Viburnums* in the chapters on "Fragrant" and "Dwarfs", but this member of the honeysuckle family must also be included for the beauty of its leaves in autumn, which turn the most rich crimson. The fruit, too, turns attractively from pale green to coral, then crimson, and finally ends a dark purple. It has white flowers in May which are rather ordinary. It was John Gerard, the surgeon, who named it in his "Herball" in the 16th century, Wayfaring Tree, because the leaves have a faint dusty look, as though they had travelled many miles along country lanes. I do not think it of enough interest to plant in the ordinary garden, but it is charming at the edge of a woodland garden, or in the shrubbery if it is large. It is useful for chalky soils where other things are fussy. Its cousin, *V. opulus* (the Water Elder or Wild Guelder Rose), is also worthy of a place in the wild garden. It is deciduous, bears snow-white flowers in June and, like *Lantana*, its full beauty is in autumn when the leaves turn bright crimson before falling. The coral fruit sometimes stays on a long time after the leaves have dropped, so giving the shrub a somewhat artificial appearance, and rather pleasing when arranged in a big vase indoors. Both these *Viburnums* grow from 6 to 12 ft. high, and the latter likes a moist place. I think the latter is the prettiest, and if the garden is large enough should certainly be included, for it gives forth a beautiful brightness at the close of the year.

Prune: not necessary.

Propagate: layering in autumn.

Xanthoceras sorbifolia (D). This is an unusual and lovely shrub, or perhaps tree is the correct term. It grows eventually up to 15 ft. if it is happy in its home. The feather-shaped leaves are a very bright green, and the flowers in May are creamy, with a red-stained centre. It is quite happy in ordinary soil, but should be in a sheltered and warm shrubbery or border.

Prune: not necessary.

Propagate: root cuttings in spring in greenhouse.

Zauschneria Californica (Californian Fuchsia). This is really a shrubby perennial, for it dies right back in winter, but in spring again it reappears with many rosy-green shoots. It is good for mixing with evergreen shrubs in the front of a border, where its absence in winter will not be noticed. It should be included if there is space, for it is a lovely thing. It grows about 1 to 1½ ft. high, and somewhat resembles musk. The tubular flowers in late September are a bright scarlet, which colour the border until the hard frosts, and are magnificent in their intensity and numbers. It likes a well-drained soil, preferably a bit sandy.

Prune: not necessary.

Propagate: cuttings in autumn, to be kept in a greenhouse until spring.

INDEX

124

English Name	See under
Cross Vine	Bignonia.
Crown Vetch	Coronilla.
Crow Berry	Empetrum.
Cypress	Cupressus.
Cucumber Tree	Magnolia.
Deer Berry	Mitchella.
Dogberry	Cornus.
Dogwood	Cornus.
Double Cherry	Prunus.
Duke of Argyll's Tea Tree	Lycium.
Dutchman's Pipe	Aristolochia.
Dwarf Almond	Prunus nana.
False Acacia	Robinia.
False Heath	Fabiana.
Firethorn	Pyracantha.
Flame Flower	Tropæolum.
Flowering Ash	Fraxinus.
Flowering Nutmeg	Leycesteria.
Fragrant Olive	Osmanthus.
French Honeysuckle	Hedysarum.
French Mulberry	Callicarpa.
Fringe Tree	Chionanthus.
Furze	Ulex.
Garland Flower	Daphne.
German Tamarix	Myricaria.
Gin Tree	Juniperus.
Ginko Tree	Ginkgo.
Goat Willow	Salix.
Golden Chain	Laburnum.
Golden Heath	Cassinia.
Gorse	Ulex.
Glory Pea	Clianthus.
Glory Tree	Clerodendron.
Grape Flower Vine	Wistaria.
Grape Pear	Amelanchier.
Grape Vine	Vitis.
Golden Ash	Fraxinus.
Ground Cistus	Rhodothamnus.
Guelder Rose	Viburnum.
Gum Cistus	Cistus.
Hawthorn	Cratægus.
Heather	Erica or Calluna.
Heath	Erica.
Heavenly Bamboo	Nandina.
Hedgehog Broom	Erinacea.
Hemp Agrimony	Eupatorium.
Herb Louisa	Lippia.
Himalayan Honeysuckle	Leycesteria.
Holly	Ilex.
Honeysuckle	Lonicera.
Honey Locust	Gleditschia.

132

English Name	See under
Silver Bell	Halesia.
Silver Birch	Betula.
Silver Fir	Abies.
Sloe	Prunus.
Smoke Tree	Rhus.
Snowball Tree	Viburnum.
Snowdrop Tree	Halesia.
Snow Flower	Chionanthus.
Snowy Mespilus	Amelanchier.
Speedwell	Veronica.
Spurge	Euphorbia.
Spruce	Pices.
Spindle Tree	Euonymus.
Spurge Laurel	Daphne.
Staff Vine	Celastrus.
Stag's Horn Sumach	Rhus.
Strawberry Tree	Arbutus.
Sumach	Rhus.
Surinam Tea Plant	Lantana.
Supple Jack	Berchemia.
Swamp Laurel	Kalmia.
Sweet Bay	Laurus.
Sweet Gale	Myrica.
Sweet Gum Tree	Liquidambar.
Sweet Fern	Comptonia.
Sweet-scented Verbena	Lippia.
Sweet Pepper Bush	Clethra.
Syringa	Philadelphus.
Syrian Mallow	Hibiscus.
Sheep Laurel	Kalmia.
Scarlet Mitre Pod	Mitraria.
Scorpion Senna	Coronilla.
South Sea Myrtle	Leptospermum.
Shrubby Althea	Hibiscus.
Southernwood	Artemesia.
Tamarisk	Tamarix.
Thorn Apple	Datura.
Tollon	Heteromelles.
Traveller's Joy	Clematis.
Tree of Heaven	Ailanthus.
Tree of the Gods	Ailanthus.
Trumpet Flower	Bignonia, Datura or Tecoma.
Tulip Tree	Liriodendron.
Tutsan	Hypericum.
Twin Flower	Linnæ.
Tea Plant	Camellia.
Victorian Snow Bush	Olearia.
Victor's Laurel	Laurus.
Virgin's Bower	Clematis.
Virginia Creeper	Vitis.